CATULLUS 68
An Interpretation

MNEMOSYNE

BIBLIOTHECA CLASSICA BATAVA

COLLEGERUNT

A. D. LEEMAN · H. W. PLEKET · W. J. VERDENIUS

BIBLIOTHECAE FASCICULOS EDENDOS CURAVIT

W. J. VERDENIUS, HOMERUSLAAN 53, ZEIST

SUPPLEMENTUM SEPTUAGESIMUM SEXTUM

JOHN SARKISSIAN

CATULLUS 68
An Interpretation

LUGDUNI BATAVORUM   E. J. BRILL   MCMLXXXIII

CATULLUS 68

An Interpretation

BY

JOHN SARKISSIAN

LEIDEN   E. J. BRILL   1983

ISBN   90 04 06939 9

PRINTED IN THE NETHERLANDS BY E. J. BRILL

CONTENTS

PREFACE

It would be futile for one attempting to analyze a complex poem such as Catullus 68 to expect certainty and presumptuous to claim it. The best the critic can do is to raise appropriate questions and offer plausible answers to them. If his readers concede the answers he provides for each question, they may then be willing to accept his interpretation of the poem as a possible one. While this is the critic's goal, he has done enough if he has stimulated his readers in a way that will assist them in reaching their own conclusions about the poem. It has been my experience that some of the studies of poem 68 with which I most strongly disagree have also been most helpful in enabling me to focus my thought and formulate the interpretation offered here.

This work began at Duke University as my doctoral dissertation. From the first I was convinced that the key to determining if the poem was a unity lay not in the seemingly insoluble philological problems, but in presenting a coherent and consistent interpretation of the poem as a whole. It seemed clear to me that the scope of the poem was such that one must treat it not as a mere occasional poem, but as one of Catullus' most serious and probing efforts. I felt that the juxtaposition of highly personal matters with Alexandrian erudition and arcane mythology and of highly figured language with plain, almost prosaic statement were of the utmost significance, but it was only over a long period of time that I was able to account to my own satisfaction for his uses of these features.

Revision of my thought did not, however, end with the completion of the dissertation, and many of the conclusions presented here differ from those I had previously come to. (Perhaps the most important change is that I now view the point of comparison when Lesbia is reintroduced at line 131 to be Protesilaus and not Laodamia, an idea first suggested to me by Professor L. Richardson, Jr.) Other changes from the dissertation include a narrowing of focus. I have omitted almost all discussion of the fascinating question of the poem's structure, since my interpretation in no way relies on structural analysis, and I have severely limited discussion of Catullan biography. I have sought to be judicious in my use of reference to the vast secondary literature. My notes and bibliography are extensive, but by no means exhaustive. In many cases, where I may seem to have cited an opposing view simply to dismiss it, my intention has been either to indicate that I am disagreeing with a generally accepted viewpoint or to call the reader's attention to another possible interpretation of the passage in question.

Much of the work on *Catullus 68: An Interpretation* was done during the Summer of 1980 at Perkins Library, Duke University, with the aid of a grant from the University Awards Program of the Research Foundation of the State of New York, for which I wish to express my gratitude, and without which completion of the work would have been long delayed. Throughout that summer I was aided by the comments, criticisms and probing questions of Professor Francis L. Newton, to whom I wish to offer my sincere thanks. I wish also to acknowledge Professor Richardson, who first stimulated my interest in Catullus, who directed my dissertation and who has subsequently read and criticized earlier drafts of this monograph with care and patience. Professor Richardson has given me far more than just his invaluable assistance on this one project.

This book is dedicated to Professor Eleanor Huzar, who has been a source of guidance and encouragement for me since my freshman year in college.

The author wishes to thank the College of Humanities and Fine Arts of the State University of New York at Albany for its generous assistance in underwriting the costs of publication of this work.

ABBREVIATIONS

References to texts and commentaries are abbreviated as follows:

Baehrens   *C. Valerius Catullus, Catulli Veronensis Liber*, ed. Emil
            Baehrens, Leipzig, 1885-1893, 2 vol. Volume 2, *Commen-
            tarium.*

Ellis   Robinson Ellis, *A Commentary on Catullus*, 2nd ed., Oxford
            1889.

Fordyce   *C. Valerius Catullus, Catullus. A Commentary*, ed. by C. J.
            Fordyce, Oxford, 1961.

Friedrich   *C. Valerius Catullus, Catulli Veronensis Liber*, ed. Gustav
            Friedrich, Leipzig, 1908.

Kroll   *C. Valerius Catullus, C. Valerius Catullus*, ed. by Wilhelm
            Kroll, 5th ed., Stuttgart, 1968.

Lenchantin *C. Valerius Catullus, Il Libro di Catullo*, ed. by Massimo
            Lenchantin de Gubernatis, Torino, 1955.

Quinn   *C. Valerius Catullus, Catullus the Poems*, ed. Kenneth Quinn,
            New York, 1970.

Periodical abbreviations are those of *L'Année Philologique*.

Ancient works and authors are abbreviated as in the *Oxford Classical Dictionary*[2] (Oxford 1972).

The text of Catullus cited here is basically that of R. A. B. Mynors (Oxford 1958).

INTRODUCTION

Poem 68 stands at the beginning of Latin love elegy. It is beyond the scope of this study to examine the specific influences it had on the subsequent development of the genre, or even to seek the predecessors that gave rise to poem 68 itself. One of the most important aspects of poem 68 for later elegy, however, has not been fully examined or appreciated and is essential to my interpretation of the poem. This has to do with the conception of an appropriate *persona* through which the poet may present the dramatic situation and express his own opinions. We have come to recognize and accept the idea of *persona* in the individual works of the other elegists,[1] but I believe that the nature and significance of the *persona* of poem 68 has eluded detection and understanding. The problem may stem from the fact that the speaker of poem 68 seems so similar to the historical Catullus, whatever position one takes on individual points of biography and chronology, and that the main topics of poem 68, the death of the brother and the relationship with Lesbia, are also topics of some of his most accessible and seemingly personal poems. It may therefore at first seem artificial and futile to insist upon a rigid distinction between the poet and the first person speaker of the poem. Without it, however, we shall miss much of the significance of poem 68.

In this study, to distinguish poet from first person voice, the former will always be referred to as "the poet," the latter always as "Catullus." Observation of the distinction permits us to regard the speaker as a less than omniscient voice, one not necessarily reliable at all times. A new dimension is added if we keep in mind that the poet is representing a narrator whose attitudes and beliefs he may not always share. This means that when Catullus says one thing, the poet, by careful control of the words and images he has Catullus use, may be saying something very different, and that we, as readers, must be on guard for instances of overstatement, wishfulness, and even self-deception and fatuousness on Catullus' part. Contradictions and ambiguities can be attributed to the speaker without therefore reflecting inconsistency on the part of the poet, whose aims may be quite different from the speaker's.

There is precedent in Hellenistic poetry for this kind of manipulation of a speaker's words to create a contrast between what the speaker asserts and what the poet actually conveys to the reader. In Theocritus and Apollonius, however, this technique is easily recognized because the speaker is always a fictional character who can in no way be confused with the poet. One of the best examples of this occurs in Theocritus' *Phar-*

maceutria (*Id.* 2), where the girl Simaetha relates the story of her romance
with Delphis. Ostensibly she is merely recalling the sequence of events
from her first view of Delphis through the consummation of the affair to
his recent abandonment of her. Within the narrative, however, there are
hints that all along the romance has been one-sided and that Simaetha
should have realized as much. She describes in great detail the ardor she
felt for Delphis (81-110) but does not seem to have observed in him any
signs of similar intensity. He looked at the ground, not at her, as he
delivered his address full of commonplaces, convincing to her but certainly not to the reader. He would have come, he said, even without a sum-
mons from Simaetha, but if so, it would have been the aftermath of a
symposium, merely a part of the night's revelry (118-28). Delphis con-
cluded with general remarks on the power of Eros rather than with
specific affirmations of his own love for Simaetha (130-34). The details
Theocritus chooses to have Simaetha remember emphasize the disparity
between her expectations and Delphis' intentions.[2] By careful control of
what is told and how it is expressed, Theocritus reveals to his reader more
about Simaetha's situation, her naivety and self-deception than the
character herself seems to understand.

Another example of Theocritus' manipulation of his speaker's words
occurs in *Id.* 11. Polyphemus, of course, is a comic figure, and the poem
contains a strong element of burlesque. Nevertheless the Cyclops engages
in introspection and self-deception similar to Simaetha's. More elaborate
is Apollonius' representation of Medea in the third book of the
Argonautica, where her emotional conflicts arising from passionate love are
explored. While Medea seems undecided about what to do, fluctuating
between indifference and grave concern for Jason, the poet, by careful
arrangement of arguments and control of vocabulary, prepares his reader
for Medea's final decision to betray her father and aid Jason, long before
she herself has determined on that course of action.

The representation of Catullus in poem 68 bears a resemblance to
these Hellenistic depictions. In the analysis of the poem that follows I
shall demonstrate that Catullus engages in introspection leading to self-
deception and that the poet, like Theocritus and Apollonius, through the
words and images he has Catullus use and the details he has him recall,
alerts the reader to Catullus' self-deception. Catullus' confusion and
disorientation for the most part are not set forth explicitly but only implied by the poet's manipulation of Catullus' words. To be sure, poem 68
depicts a situation more complex and realistic than any of the Greek
poems do, and the depth of self-examination is much greater. I should
not argue for anything approaching direct imitation here, but it is not
unlikely that the type of representation contained in these poems con-
tributed to the genesis of 68.[3]

The distinction of poet and speaker in poem 68 is complicated by the fact that the speaker, Catullus, is also a poet. In 68a,[4] the poet has represented Catullus as replying to the letter of a friend, but in 68b he represents him as composing a poem for that friend. The abrupt and unmistakable change in tone between 68a and 68b dramatizes this change in Catullus from correspondent to poet in the heat of composition. Here it becomes even more crucial that the reader not lose sight of the distinction between poet and speaker; for, as will be shown below, Catullus often employs the conventions of poetry intending to achieve one effect, while the poet, operating on another level, manipulates Catullus' language in order to achieve quite a different one.

To illustrate the advantage of distinguishing the poet from Catullus in the analysis of the poem, I should like here to consider just one passage, formulating the kinds of questions encouraged by a close reading of the text. Even a partial answer to these will indicate how I intend to proceed in my analysis. After the long digression on Laodamia, Catullus returns to Lesbia upon her entrance to the house in which he awaits her (131-40):

> aut nihil aut paulo cui tum concedere digna
>   lux mea se nostrum contulit in gremium,
> quam circumcursans hinc illinc saepe Cupido
>   fulgebat crocina candidus in tunica.
> quae tamen etsi uno non est contenta Catullo,
>   rara verecundae furta feremus erae,
> ne nimium simus stultorum more molesti.
>   saepe etiam Iuno, maxima caelicolum,
> coniugis in culpa flagrantem concoquit iram,
>   noscens omnivoli plurima furta Iovis.

Why is Lesbia now being compared with Protesilaus?[5] What is the meaning of the fanciful notion that Cupid, dressed in a saffron tunic more appropriate to Hymen,[6] attends her? How should the reader account for the sudden change from this highly idealized picture of Lesbia to the revelation of her infidelity? How can Catullus call Lesbia *verecunda*?[7] What are the implications of *era*? What is the force of the mythological exemplum? Can Catullus really assume this nonchalance toward the woman he has described in such glowing terms? How can lines 135-40 be reconciled with what has preceded in the poem?[8]

When the passage is read with the distinction of poet and speaker in mind the poet's motives become intelligible. Catullus as composer of a poem (68b) idealizes his beloved, exaggerating her attractive qualities. Such idealization accords well with the tone of Catullus' poem in high epic style, with invocation of the Muses, apostrophe of the gods, elaborate imagery and mythological exemplum. At line 130, however, reality begins to intrude upon the poetic exercise. Catullus continues to praise his beloved, but the images the poet has him employ are somewhat disquieting. The comparison of Lesbia to Protesilaus carries with it the implication that Catullus' affair with Lesbia, like the reunion of Laodamia and Protesilaus, is to be short-lived and end in tragedy. Cupid's saffron tunic, a garment proper to Hymen, underscores that Catullus and Lesbia are not husband and wife, as Catullus would have liked. Immediately after this remarkably idealized vision of the god in attendance upon the mortal woman, the burden of Lesbia's infidelity intrudes into Catullus' depiction. He admits openly that there are others, but in pretending indifference is betrayed by his own words. *verecundae* seems preposterous, and *erae* amounts to an admission of his inferior position. He tries to improve things by use of a mythological exemplum, but the choice is a poor one. Juno is not nonchalant but swallows her impotent anger out of fear. Furthermore Jupiter is hardly appropriate for comparison with one described as *verecunda*.

The poet, under no obligation to tell the complete truth, would have been perfectly free to ignore Lesbia's infidelity and to continue the idealization to the very end of the poem. He must have anticipated the jarring and disturbing effect of its introduction at this point in the poem, and his reasons for including it must be more substantial than merely some scruple about adhering to the truth. What in fact the poet achieves here, in dramatic fashion, is a representation of Catullus as attempting and failing to conceal his unhappiness under the veil of poetic elaboration and idealization. We see the façade crumble as Catullus passes from idealization to reality then to rationalization and (by line 148) grim insistence in the face of the inescapable truth. Thus while Catullus may display poor judgment in speaking of Lesbia's infidelity, and poor choice of words (*verecundae erae*) and exemplum, the poet succeeds brilliantly in depicting Catullus' miserable failure at self-deception.

The interpretation of the poem offered here relies heavily on this distinction of the poet and the first person speaker Catullus to elucidate several difficult passages in which I suggest that Catullus speaks on one level and the poet on another, more informed level. For the poet ultimately controls the speaker's language and thereby delineates his character and psychology in greater clarity than Catullus' words taken at face value can do.

At this point I should note that my insistence on distinguishing the poet from the speaker Catullus does not prevent my acceptance of the traditional Catullan biography and chronology.[9] I subscribe to the view that the woman of poem 68 is Lesbia, that Lesbia was Clodia Metelli, and that most, if not all, of the Lesbia poems originate in actual experience. I should include poem 68 among these but with the qualification that there is a chronological distance between the time represented in the poem and the time of its composition. If the poet is able to depict Catullus engaging in self-deception, he himself must have attained a superior awareness and objectivity. Thus while some of the Lesbia poems may have been written close to the time they depict in the relationship, e.g., poem 5 could well have been composed while the affair with Lesbia was fresh and exhilarating and poem 11 at the time of a final, or seemingly final, separation, it seems highly unlikely that poem 68 could have been written at precisely the time in the relationship which it represents.

Anyone attempting an interpretation of poem 68 is confronted with a massive volume of criticism. The poem has received more scholarly attention than any other in the Catullan corpus. The numerous textual and philological problems have been discussed and debated in more than a hundred articles and books.[10] The difficulty of some of these problems and the complexity and originality of the poem have made it a constant and attractive object of new studies. The volume of scholarship has not, however, resulted in a general consensus on many of the philological problems, on the question of the unity or disunity of the poem, or even on its quality as a work of literature. Many pertinent, even essential, questions have never been properly raised, let alone answered, and there is still need for a comprehensive and convincing interpretation of the poem as a whole.[11] My intention is to pose the questions that must be answered if such an interpretation is ever to be achieved and to try to fill that need.

Most of the work on poem 68 is concerned with textual problems, structure, interpretation of individual passages and ultimately the question of unity. Scholars have concentrated on the following six problems: 1) the name of the addressee or addressees, since the manuscripts are contradictory on this point; 2) the cause of the distress of the addressee of 68a and the nature of the *Munera et Musarum et Veneris* which he requests; 3) the text and meaning of lines 27-30; 4) the proper case and the meaning of *domina* in line 69; 5) the identity of the person referred to in lines 157-58; 6) the schema that best delineates the structural pattern of the poem. The overriding question, of course, is whether 68 is one poem or two.

To some extent these problems are interrelated, and the solution to one may determine that of another. Thus if one supports a solution to the problem of the addressee's name that distinguishes the recipient of 68a from the dedicatee of 68b, one is likely to argue for two distinct poems. Conversely, one convinced for other reasons of the poem's unity will insist on a solution to the problem of the name which is compatible with that unity. So, too, any explanation of the friend's distress and his re-

quest for *munera et Musarum et Veneris* must be consistent with the interpretation of lines 27-30, where it is declared shameful that either Catullus
or his friend should be in Verona while somewhere someone warms cold
limbs in an abandoned bed. The other problems listed above do admit of
more independent solutions, although some of the proposed structural
schemata have a bearing on the question of unity.

It is neither to deny the importance of these matters nor to avoid grap-
pling with them that I shall treat them as secondary issues. While my goal
of formulating a comprehensive interpretation of the poem necessitates
my offering some solutions to each of these problems, except that of structure,[12] long argumentation on every issue would only detract from my
main purpose. Furthermore much of what I would have to say on these
matters would be repetition of arguments already advanced by others.
For example, on the question of the addressee's name I have accepted a
variation on the solution offered by Schoell, but the only argument I have
to bolster his case or to refute the conjectures of others is my interpretation of the poem, which requires that it be a unity addressed to a single
person.[13] For the most part I will relegate discussion of critical and
philological problems to footnotes, acknowledging there my debt to the
many scholars whose efforts have cleared the way for this contribution to
our understanding of the poem.

Before beginning a line by line examination of the poem, I offer the
following synopsis which will serve to orient the reader and to indicate
my interpretation of the difficult and controversial passages. At the
poem's start Catullus addresses his friend Allius in response to a letter he
has received from him. Allius, upset by a temporary separation from his
mistress and unable to sleep, has asked Catullus to come to him and rally
his spirits and also to bring with him some new verses (*munera et Musarum
et Veneris*, 10). Catullus replies that he cannot help. His brother's death
has left him prostrate, and he has now abandoned the pursuits of his
carefree youth (11-20). He interrupts his address to Allius to apos-
trophize his brother in a dirge (20-24). Returning to Allius, Catullus
quotes verbatim his friend's complaint: it is a shame that Catullus should
linger in Verona when Allius, languishing in a bed abandoned by his
beloved, has need of him. Not shameful, Catullus replies, but merely
pitiable (27-30). Further he explains that because he is not now in Rome,
his real home, he has but few books with him and so does not even have
appropriate poetry to send to Allius (31-36). He repeats his apology,
assuring Allius that he would do more for him if he were able (37-40).
Then unexpectedly Catullus changes course, exclaiming that he cannot
keep quiet about Allius' service to him, that he intends to immortalize his
friend's name in verse (41-50). He explains in elaborate imagery that
Allius helped him in a difficult love affair. When tears were streaming

down Catullus' cheeks like a stream flowing down from a mountain, Allius provided relief like the relief a stream brings to a weary traveler or a favorable breeze to a storm-tossed sailor (51-66). Allius, in fact, provided Catullus with a house in which he could meet Lesbia and a mistress of the house whose presence would cloak their rendezvous in respectability (67-69). Referring to Lesbia as his *candida diva*, Catullus reconstructs her first coming to him with emphasis on small details such as her stepping on the threshold (70-72). He compares her to Laodamia, the wife of Protesilaus, the first Greek to die at Troy, and digresses on Laodamia herself (73-86). The mention of Troy (87-90) reminds Catullus of his brother's death there, and the poem is interrupted by a lament for and apostrophe of the dead brother (91-100), in which lines are repeated from the earlier lament. Catullus then returns to the Trojan War and Laodamia. He compares the depth of her despair at the loss of her husband with the depth of a channel dug by Hercules, concluding that Laodamia's love was deeper than this channel (105-18). Protesilaus returning to her from the Underworld was as dear to her as a late-born heir is to his grandfather (119-24), and her passion on that occasion exceeded that of a dove for her mate (125-30). Finally Lesbia reappears, this time likened to Protesilaus. When she came to the house, Catullus asserts, Cupid accompanied her (131-34). He acknowledges that she is not always faithful to him but resolves to endure the *rara furta* of his *verecundae erae*. He cites as a precedent that Juno often swallowed her anger in the face of Jupiter's misconduct (135-42). Furthermore Lesbia is not his wife but rather was the wife of another when they met at the house. He will be content then if she considers the days she spends with him to be her best (143-48). Addressing Allius again, Catullus offers him the poem (149-54) and concludes with a benediction asked for all those who have played a part in it, Allius and his beloved, the *domus* and the mistress of the *domus*, Catullus' brother and, above all, Lesbia *qua viva* living is sweet for Catullus.

I regard poem 68 as in part an attempt, greatly affected by the death of Catullus' brother, to put the love affair with Lesbia into perspective. I feel, however, that the poem also deals with a larger issue, the relationship between the world of art as a poet may represent it and the world of reality as he perceives it. The poet's depiction of Catullus in the act of composing a poem constitutes an exploration of the conflict, often irreconcilable, between the world a poet can create and fashion as he likes and the world in which he sees himself as living and over which he feels he can exert little control. The passage discussed above is only one instance of the dramatization of this dichotomy; time and again in poem 68 we will see that the realities of Catullus' life, his disintegrating affair with Lesbia and the death of his brother, intrude upon and subvert his attempts to create a poetic perfection.

CATULLUS 68

The poem begins with an exaggerated picture of grief and suffering, apparently quoted or paraphrased from Allius' letter to Catullus (1-10):

> quod mihi fortuna casuque oppressus acerbo
> conscriptum hoc lacrimis mittis epistolium,
> naufragum ut eiectum spumantibus aequoris undis
> sublevem et a mortis limine restituam,
> quem neque sancta Venus molli requiescere somno
> desertum in lecto caelibe perpetitur,
> nec veterum dulci scriptorum carmine Musae
> oblectant, cum mens anxia pervigilat:
> id gratum est mihi, me quoniam tibi dicis amicum,
> muneraque et Musarum hinc petis et Veneris.

Allius, ship-wrecked, overboard at the height of the storm, at the threshold of death, sends Catullus a tear-stained plea for help. The third and fourth couplets explain in general terms the course of Allius' anguish. At first glance lines 5-6 and 7-8 appear to be parallel, and this impression is reinforced by the linking of Venus and the Muses in line 10. A close reading, however, shows that Venus is the cause of Allius' troubles and that the failure of literature to distract him is only a secondary consideration. Venus actively makes Allius' life miserable, not allowing him to sleep (*perpetitur*), while the Muses merely fail to please him (*oblectant*). Furthermore from the *cum*-temporal clause of line 8 it is clear that only in wakefulness caused by Venus does Allius turn to the Muses for solace.[14] In these dire straits Allius asks Catullus for *munera et Musarum et Veneris*, that he visit him and rally his spirits and that he either bring along or send poetry that might capture Allius' fancy as the familiar literature he has at hand has failed to do.[15]

Although some find the first ten lines of the poem so bitterly and intensely serious as to suggest that the addressee's wife or mistress has died,[16] a strong case can be made for viewing them as deliberate literary overstatement not to be taken at face value.[17] Three indications of this are the request of lines 9-10, Catullus' reply (11-14), and the reference to Allius' beloved as *tua vita* at the conclusion of the poem (155).[18] However one interprets *munera et Musarum et Veneris*, it is difficult to reconcile this request with bereavement over the death of a loved one or some other equally serious catastrophe, and the inclusion of Allius' *vita* in the closing benediction is a further indication that the crisis is merely a temporary separation or quarrel. Most persuasive, however, is the answer Catullus makes in refusing to comply with Allius' request (11-14):

> sed tibi ne mea sint ignota incommoda, mi Alli,
> neu me odisse putes hospitis officium,
> accipe quis merser fortunae fluctibus ipse,
> ne amplius a misero dona beata petas.

In introducing his own misfortunes, Catullus appropriates Allius' sea metaphor and even outdoes his correspondent. Whereas Allius was merely tossed in the waves, Catullus actually goes under (*merser*). The imperative *accipe*, the intensive *ipse* and *quis fluctibus*, implying waves of a different quality from Allius', all contribute to the impression that Catullus' difficulties are greater and more serious than his friend's. Such a reply would be selfish and brutal were Allius bereaved by death, for, although concerned that he not seem churlish, neither here nor elsewhere in the poem does Catullus commiserate with his friend.[19] If this absence of sympathy is not to be attributed to gross insensitivity on Catullus' part, it must stem from the fact that Allius' condition is not truly desperate.

Rather the elaborate simile, metaphor and other imagery with which the poem begins are all part of a conscious overstatement, a dramatization of the plight of the typical lover, and it is only in his own view and description that Allius is gravely afflicted. The poet wishes to invoke and impress upon the reader the tenor of a lover's lament, which may then serve as a foil to Catullus' sober lament over the death of his brother (20-24). Below I shall examine the striking contrast between the stark language of that lament and the richness of the language of Allius' complaint.

This passage contains two thematically important images, that of the storm-tossed sailor, which will be repeated when Catullus speaks of the early stages of his affair with Lesbia (63-66) and that of the *hospitis officium*, the importance of which remains a mystery until Catullus reveals that Allius provided a house in which he and Lesbia could meet.

Delaying exposition of the source of his own distress, Catullus explains that he is miserably drained of both the youthful exuberance and the creative energy needed to comply with Allius' requests. He once possessed both in abundance, but the death of his brother has driven from his mind all the pursuits of his youth (15-20):

> tempore quo primum vestis mihi tradita pura est,
> iucundum cum aetas florida ver ageret,
> multa satis lusi: non est dea nescia nostri,
> quae dulcem curis miscet amaritiem.
> sed totum hoc studium luctu fraterna mihi mors
> abstulit.

ludere is commonly used in reference to love affairs and also to the writing of love poetry.[20] Both meanings are possible here, and it is likely that the poet chose this ambiguous word to encompass both.[21] *non est dea nescia nostri* should indicate that Catullus had his share of romantic adventures but could also be taken as a reference to love poetry which would likewise attract Venus' attention. The other words used to characterize Catullus' youth are similarly imprecise: *studium* (19) and later *studia* and *delicias animi* (26). *deliciae*, like *ludere*, is a suitable word for either poetry on erotic themes or love affairs themselves.[22]

vestis pura here is curious and significant. Propertius (3.18.3-4) indicates that upon assumption of the *toga virilis* a young man obtained freedom to get involved with members of the opposite sex. Catullus took advantage of this liberty and the ambiguous *multa satis lusi* is an appropriate way to designate the parties and flirtations he would have engaged in. But the *toga virilis* was assumed about the age of sixteen and the Catullus of poem 68, by any chronology, must be twenty-five, if not thirty. While one need not expect an abrupt abandonment of such pursuits, it is interesting that the activities of a more mature period of his life should be lumped together with those of his late adolescence. The implication is that in light of his brother's death Catullus has come to regard all his former behavior as frivolous and childish.[23] The only exception, upon which Catullus will later insist, is the relationship with Lesbia. The poet, however, operating on a more informed level, will provide, through vocabulary and imagery, which echo the first twenty lines, indications that this relationship too is a thing of the past, a youthful indulgence that has got out of hand.

The mention of the death of Catullus' brother inspires an apostrophe that confirms the depth of his sorrow (20-24):

> o misero frater adempte mihi,
> tu mea tu moriens fregisti commoda, frater,
> tecum una tota est nostra sepulta domus;
> omnia tecum una perierunt gaudia nostra,
> quae tuus in vita dulcis alebat amor.

By beginning the apostrophe in the middle of the second line of a couplet, the poet dramatizes the spontaneity and anguish of Catullus' outburst. At the thought of his brother Catullus cannot restrain himself. *tota est nostra sepulta domus* (22) here seems simply to mean that the death has brought an enormous sense of sorrow and loss to the family. When the same lament is repeated later in the poem, however, the reader will be in a better position to appreciate the force of *sepulta domus* in light of what has been learned about the *domus* provided by Allius, in which Catullus and Lesbia began their now deteriorating relationship.

The contrast between Allius' mere disappointment in a love affair and Catullus' serious and permanent loss is underscored by the difference in the language used to describe the two situations. Allius' condition is the subject of elaborate imagery whereas, except for the rather stark metaphor of the buried house, Catullus' outburst is devoid of poetic ornamentation. This is the first of several passages in which the poet sets up a sharp contrast between the poetic embellishments used to depict one situation and the grim realities of another. Here we see that mere separation from one's mistress may be dressed up to sound like high tragedy, but expression of true grief cannot be aided by poetic ornamentation.

Reiterating his changed state of mind, Catullus returns to Allius' letter, quoting directly from it (25-30):

> cuius ego interitu tota de mente fugavi
>   haec studia atque omnes delicias animi.
> quare, quod scribis: "Veronae turpe, Catulle,
>   esse, quod hic quisquis de meliore nota
> frigida deserto tepefecit membra cubili."
>   id mi, Alli, non est turpe, magis miserum est.

"It is a shame," Allius has written, "for you, Catullus, to be in Verona when here a good man (like myself) is trying vainly to warm cold limbs in a bed that has been abandoned by his beloved."[24]

We must assume that Allius' reproach, like his initial complaint, is not entirely serious, but that in asking Catullus to come to him he has good-naturedly chided him for his absence. The spirit of the reproach would be like that of Catullus 38, where Cornificius is charged with failure to console Catullus.[25] The juxtaposition of *turpe* and *miserum* in Catullus' reply is striking. As Allius' condition, that of the typical lover, has been contrasted with Catullus' graver situation, so here Allius' accusation, made light-heartedly in ignorance, that Catullus' inaction is shameful, is undercut by the straightforward reply.

Catullus offers another excuse for his inability to provide *munera Musarum* (31-36):

> ignosces igitur si, quae mihi luctus ademit,
>   haec tibi non tribuo munera, cum nequeo.
> nam, quod scriptorum non magna est copia apud me,
>   hoc fit, quod Romae vivimus: illa domus,
> illa mihi sedes, illic mea carpitur aetas;
>   huc una ex multis capsula me sequitur.

Catullus, having already explained that his state of mind will not permit him to compose, now adds that he does not even have anything appropriate with him that he might send. *copia scriptorum* may refer to poems by Catullus, poems by other authors, or a combination of the two, some of which Catullus would send to Allius if he could.[26] Apparently the *capsula* brought to Verona contained writings already familiar or otherwise useless to Allius.[27]

In lines 34-35 Catullus emphasizes that Rome is his true home. The idea of home is repeated (*domus*, *sedes*). Catullus lives there (*vivimus*) and there his life culls its flower (*mea carpitur aetas*). With this phrase the poet takes us back to Catullus' youth (*iucundum cum aetas florida ver ageret*, 16), and *domus* calls to mind the *sepulta domus* of line 22. Catullus' insistence that Rome is his home is too vehement to have been touched off by the mere mention of his books, and the poet is certainly not simply having him inform Allius and the reader of what they already know. With the echoes of lines 16 and 22, the poet reminds the reader that by Catullus' own admission it is no longer spring for him, and his *domus* is now *sepulta*. Catullus, however, insists on using the present tense in lines 34-35 in speaking of what he himself has just said are things of his young and frivolous past, betraying thus an emotional conflict, an awareness of loss mingled with an unwillingness to accept the loss.[28] The lack of a *magna copia scriptorum* and the presence of just *capsula una ex multis* symbolize the change. He is out of his element now, and one indication is his separation from the books that had once been an integral part of his life.

Catullus concludes with a reiteration of his helplessness and his regret at being unable to accommodate his friend (37-40):

> quod cum ita sit, nolim statuas nos mente maligna
>   id facere aut animo non satis ingenuo,
> quod tibi non utriusque petenti copia posta est:
>   ultro ego deferrem, copia siqua foret.

Catullus must be saying that he can fulfil neither part of the request.[29] The whole thrust of 68a is that grief has incapacitated him, and there has been no indication anywhere of even partial compliance with Allius' demands. That the poem continues after line 40 is irrelevant. Line 41 constitutes a new beginning, anticipated, of course, by the poet, but not by Catullus. At line 40 Catullus has said all that he has to say and is concluding his verse epistle.

68a introduces three important ideas that recur later in the poem. The contrast between Allius' misfortune in a love affair, made to sound tragic and fatal, and Catullus' far more serious loss of his brother, lamented in plain language largely free from poetic elaboration, constitutes the first of several dramatizations of the dichotomy between the world that can be represented in verse by studied use of poetic devices and the realities of life which cannot be altered or much mitigated by poetry. Second the profound change in Catullus from carefree youth to more serious, sober perception has been established. Catullus has not entirely reconciled himself to these changes as lines 34-35 indicate and as some of his later assertions about Lesbia will confirm. Finally the image of the *domus* has made its first appearances in the poem. Catullus' *domus* has been buried, although he still insists that it exists for him in Rome. The next time the *domus* is mentioned it will be learned that the house is that in which Catullus and Lesbia conducted their once happy but now foundering love affair.

At line 41 the poem undergoes a remarkable change in tone and content (41-50):

> non possum reticere, deae, qua me Allius in re
>   iuverit aut quantis iuverit officiis,
> ne fugiens saeclis obliviscentibus aetas
>   illius hoc caeca nocte tegat studium:
> sed dicam vobis, vos porro dicite multis
>   milibus et facite haec carta loquatur anus.
> ....
> notescatque magis mortuus atque magis,
> nec tenuem texens sublimis aranea telam
>   in deserto Alli nomine opus faciat.

The epistle addressed to and ostensibly for one person now becomes a public proclamation, elevated in tone and rich in texture.

The abrupt transition between lines 40 and 41 is best explained by assuming a pause,[30] to represent a moment of reflection. As Catullus concludes his apology, his thoughts turn from his present misery to the happiness of former times. He recalls the *hospitis officium* Allius once performed for him and which he has just mentioned (12). Inspired by these memories, he begins anew with an expression of thanks. This fresh enthusiasm comes out in the exclamation *non possum reticere*. The impression given is that his desire to celebrate Allius has supplanted, at least temporarily, his grief over the death of his brother.

The change in tone is, of course, completely self-conscious on the poet's part. From line 41 on, in effect, Catullus is himself in the process of composing a poem in honor of his friend Allius. Indications of this are the formal invocation of the Muses, which is a stock feature of narrative and encomiastic poetry, and the wealth of imagery.

The length and fervor of the declaration are striking. The enthusiasm of lines 41-42 is amplified in a series of images, not individually extravagant, but forceful in their quick succession. Catullus will not allow the passage of time to shroud Allius' *studium* with blind night. He will speak directly to the Muses, who are then to carry the message to thousands more.[31] Even in its old age the *carta* will celebrate Allius.[32] The spider's web will not obscure his name. The repetition of the same idea in varied images reinforces the feeling of conviction and determination expressed in line 41.

Catullus delays revealing exactly what Allius' service was, setting forth only in very broad terms the situation in which Allius aided him (51-56):

> nam, mihi quam dederit duplex Amathusia curam,
>   scitis, et in quo me corruerit genere,
> cum tantum arderem quantum Trinacria rupes
>   lymphaque in Oetaeis Malia Thermopylis,
> maesta neque assiduo tabescere lumina fletu
>   cessarent tristique imbre madere genae,

Geographical erudition, simile, metaphor and Homeric elaboration combine to make the tone of this passage lofty to the point of high artificiality. Venus is identified by the name of a city on Cyprus, and the heat of Catullus' passion is compared first to that of Mount Aetna, obliquely described as the Trinacrian crag,[33] then to the hot springs at Thermopylae. His cheeks are drenched in an unabating torrent of tears. *scitis*, addressed to the Muses, conforms with the Homeric idea of attributing to those goddesses knowledge of all past history[34] and complements the conventional invocation of line 41.

Lines 51-52 contain echoes of earlier passages. Venus is here the cause of Catullus' discomfort as she had been of Allius'. She did not allow Allius to sleep; she gives Catullus *cura* and brings him crashing down.[35] There are also echoes of lines 17-18 where Catullus describes his youth. *duplex* is a fitting epithet for the goddess *quae dulcem curis miscet amaritiem* (18), and here again Venus is a dispenser of *curae*. By these verbal echoes the poet strikes a discordant note even as he introduces one of the major themes of the poem, Catullus' relationship with Lesbia. Catullus presents this affair, in which Allius aided him, in dramatic language, rich in imagery. Concealed in this language, however, is the implication that the affair is like Allius' and like Catullus' youthful *lusus*, that as such it pales in significance when juxtaposed with the death of his brother, and that it should, like his other youthful escapades, now be put aside. Thus the poet lays the groundwork for the subsequent admission of Lesbia's infidelity and of the deterioration of their relationship. The reader, warned well in advance that Catullus is actually describing a thing of the past, is prepared to view with scepticism Catullus' insistence at the conclusion of the poem that all is well.

To the already elaborate description of Catullus' condition is added an extended simile (57-62):

> qualis in aerii perlucens vertice montis
>   rivus muscoso prosilit e lapide,

> qui cum de prona praeceps est valle volutus,
>   per medium densi transit iter populi,
> dulce viatori lasso in sudore levamen,
>   cum gravis exustos aestus hiulcat agros,

The first impression is that Catullus' tears of line 55-56 are being compared to a mountain cascade, but as the relief that the stream brings a weary traveler is brought into focus, it appears that this simile, along with the ensuing one (63-65), describes rather the assistance Allius gave to Catullus (*tale fuit nobis Allius auxilium*, 66). In fact, the simile describes both Catullus' tears and Allius' *auxilium*.[36] There is precedent for such similes in Homer and in Apollonius Rhodius,[37] and the device is quite in keeping with the conscious artifice of 68b. Moreover, the river simile has a parallel in the *barathrum* simile of the Laodamia passage (107-18), which quite clearly describes both what precedes it and what follows. The initial point of comparison there is the depth of sorrow into which Laodamia was plunged, but the final point is the depth of her love. Both are compared to the depth of the channel which Hercules dug. The interrelation of the river simile and the *barathrum* simile is reinforced by the studied contrast between the two, the one a fresh stream flowing down from a mountain, the other a channel dug through a mountain to drain stagnant, noisome water from a swamp. Furthermore just as the *barathrum* simile makes a transition from distress to happiness, from Laodamia's grief at the loss of her husband to her love for him at his return, so the river simile, starts with Catullus' tears and concludes with Allius' assistance.[38]

The river simile is followed by yet another simile (63-66):

> ac[39] velut in nigro iactatis turbine nautis
>   lenius aspirans aura secunda venit
> iam prece Pollucis, iam Castoris implorata
>   tale fuit nobis Allius auxilium.

The image here recalls the opening lines of the poem where Allius is identified as a ship-wrecked sailor (*iactatis/eiectum*). This time, however, the sailors' prayers are answered. The contrast is obvious: Allius once helped Catullus in similar difficulties, but circumstances have made it impossible for Catullus to reciprocate. More importantly, the allusion to the earlier passage serves to link Catullus' love affair once again with Allius', with the implication that Catullus' affair, too, should be of less importance compared to the death of his brother.

Finally at line 67, after twenty-six lines of preamble, Catullus tells us exactly what Allius did for him (67-69):

> is clausum lato patefecit limite campum,
>   isque domum nobis isque dedit dominam
> ad quam communes exerceremus amores.

Allius opened a closed field, in that he provided Catullus with the opportunity to pursue his romance with Lesbia.[40] Specifically Allius provided a
house in which Catullus and Lesbia could meet and a housewife, whose
presence would shield the liaison behind a facade of respectability.[41] This
domina, well-disposed toward the couple, would have been the mistress of
the house at which Catullus and Lesbia gave scope to their love for each
other (*communes amores*).[42]

As with the excessively ornate description of Allius' distress at the start
of the poem, here again poetic elaboration is shown to bear little relation
to objective reality. These three lines illustrate dramatically the central
conflict of the poem, the dichotomy between the world a poet can create
and the world in which he lives. The poet presents us with a situation in
which Catullus' poetic response to a commonplace action is markedly in-
congruent with our realistic assessment of it. The pedestrian, rather sordid nature of Allius' generosity undercuts the lofty tone in which it has
been approached. Allius' *auxilium* is the sort of thing one should keep
quiet about, certainly nothing to record for posterity.[43] The poet shows
that although Catullus employs epic convention and rich imagery to
celebrate his friend, in the end Allius' gesture was not particularly noble.
When later in the poem Lesbia is praised in glowing terms and elevated
to the rank of goddess only to be exposed as unfaithful and promiscuous,
it will become clearer that Catullus is attempting both here with regard to
Allius and there with regard to Lesbia to foist off upon the realities of his
love affair the lofty nobility and heroism appropriate to an unattainable
ideal. The poet depicts Catullus attempting to retreat from an unsatisfactory reality into the world of poetry in which he seeks to shape events as
he wants them.

Lesbia's entry into the house is announced in lines remarkable for the
detail in which Catullus recreates an isolated moment (70-72):

> quo mea se molli candida diva pede
> intulit et trito fulgentem in limine plantam
> innixa arguta constituit solea,

The idealization of Lesbia begins with her introduction as *candida diva*,
shining, beautiful goddess.[44] The use of *diva* of the beloved woman is extraordinary. It was not picked up by Propertius or Tibullus and the two
times Ovid uses it, the contexts are quite different from this.[45] Lesbia's
foot is *mollis*, an indication of the delicacy of one unaccustomed to the
roughness of the streets and perhaps a reference to the gracefulness of her

walk.[46] In the next line her foot (*plantam*) is further described as *fulgentem*. The threshold on which she steps is *trito*, either because it is worn down or because it is polished.[47] In any case the *limen* provides a background against which the delicate foot stands out. The participle *innixa* and the main verb *constituit* prolong the moment of her entrance. As Lesbia steps on the threshold another sense, that of hearing, is called into play, *arguta solea* marking the sharp, clear sound her sandal makes at the moment of contact.[48] That Catullus has such a clear recollection of minute details indicates the importance of this meeting for him.

In this charming description, however, there is a grim foreboding. Lesbia steps not over but directly on the threshold, and this act is emphasized by *constituit* and *innixa*. Certain elements in Lesbia's coming to the house invite the reader to view the meeting as a symbolic marriage. Catullus is apparently waiting in the house as the groom would await his bride, and Cupid, who accompanies Lesbia (133-34) is dressed in saffron as one might expect the marriage god Hymen to be (see above, n. 6). In Roman marriage ceremony it was considered ill-omened for the new bride to come into contact with any part of the door frame as she entered her husband's house.[49] The almost casual detail of Lesbia's stepping on the threshold introduces a sinister element into an otherwise delightful scene and undercuts Catullus' climactic moment of triumph. He dresses up that moment in glorious imagery and extols his beloved as a goddess, but at the same time, operating on a symbolic level, the poet warns us that Catullus and Lesbia are already moving toward the ultimately bitter and miserable conclusion of their affair.[50]

Lesbia is then compared to the mythological heroine Laodamia, an unusual choice since Laodamia is a relatively unimportant figure in mythology and her story ultimately a tragic and shocking one.[51]

Protesilaus, the first Greek killed in the Trojan War, left behind on their wedding night his new bride Laodamia in a house which Homer describes as ἡμιτελής, "half-finished."[52] Even in antiquity there was disagreement about whether the adjective meant literally that Protesilaus had been building a house when he left for Troy or figuratively that the marriage had been disrupted before any offspring was produced (Eust., *Il.* 325 [2.701]). In some accounts Laodamia commits suicide immediately upon hearing of her husband's death.[53] In other versions she remains faithful to him even after his death and the infernal gods permit them a brief reunion.[54] Laodamia's suicide then follows upon Protesilaus' second departure. Eustathius (*Il.* 325) adds the detail that out of loyalty to her dead husband she refuses her father's request that she remarry.

Other variations take on a bizarre and macabre character. In these Laodamia on learning of Protesilaus' death makes a likeness of him from which she obtains sexual gratification.[55] Sometimes in a clumsy effort to reconcile the two versions, the fashioning of the image is made a preliminary to Protesilaus' return from the Underworld.[56] According to Hyginus (*Fab.* 104) the image is made after Protesilaus' second departure. In any case Laodamia's father, on discovery of the image, burns it, and Laodamia, in a fit of passion and despair, destroys herself by following it into the flames. Even this condensed survey shows that Laodamia could serve as an example either of loyal devotion or of ardent sexual passion. In the discussion of the Laodamia passage here, I have assumed that the reader of poem 68 would have had a thorough knowledge of all variations of the myth and that such knowledge is essential to an understanding of the force of the comparison first with Lesbia and subsequently with Catullus himself.

The Laodamia simile invites contrast with Lesbia as well as comparison and, on close examination, proves to be fraught with unpleasant implications (73-76):

> coniugis ut quondam flagrans advenit amore
>   Protesilaeam Laudamia domum
> inceptam frustra, nondum cum sanguine sacro
>   hostia caelestis pacificasset eros.

The obvious point of comparison is that both women are coming to houses in which their lovers await them, but with the significant difference that Laodamia goes as a proper bride to her husband's house. The word order of the first couplet calls attention to this difference in most striking fashion. Line 73, *coniugis ut quondam flagrans advenit amore*, could constitute a complete thought, and while an accusative to complete *advenit* might be anticipated, the reader need not have expected to find a subject for the verb in line 74. Indeed until the reader comes to the nominative *Laudamia* in that line, the subject seems to be the *candida diva* of line 70. If this were the case, however, the sense would be that Lesbia came to Catullus burning with love as she once burned with love for her husband. Line 74, of course, makes it clear that *ut* is introducing a mythological simile, but the poet has momentarily produced the impression that Catullus is actually speaking here of Lesbia's husband. Catullus himself is merely comparing Lesbia to Laodamia, but the word order the poet has him use exposes a serious flaw in their relationship, namely that she was the wife of another. The point is emphasized throughout the Laodamia passage by repetition of words concerned with legitimate marriage (*coniugis*, 73 and 81; *coniugio*, 84; *coniugium*, 107; *viro*, 80 and 130) and by images of married couples and family life (Hercules and Hebe, 115-16; the monogamous doves, 125-28; the grandfather who welcomes a late-born heir, 119-24).⁵⁷ The marriage of Protesilaus and Laodamia is not, however, entirely proper. It is not consummated until Protesilaus' return from the dead and, as lines 79-86 indicate, certain aspects of the marriage ritual were neglected. The suggestion is not only that Catullus' relationship with Lesbia is not a legitimate marriage, but that, even to the extent that it can be construed as a symbolic one, it is flawed. The Laodamia passage thus serves as a preparation for Catullus' admission later in the poem that Lesbia is not faithful to him, that she was, in fact, the wife of another, and that he has little claim on her (143-46).

The only phrase describing Laodamia in lines 73-76, *flagrans amore*, hints at another serious problem in Catullus' relationship with Lesbia. This is surely a *double-entendre* intended to remind the reader of the Laodamia who actually burns in the fire in which her father has destroyed the image of Protesilaus. Thus without actually introducing it into the poem, the poet calls attention to the strangest variation of the myth, and the simile takes a sinister turn. It is quite reasonable to compare one's beloved to a mythological figure known for her beauty or to an exemplar of faithfulness, which Laodamia is in some versions of the myth. But with *flagrans amore* the poet speaks of a Laodamia who epitomizes passion rather than faithfulness, an unnatural passion at that. On the surface Catullus is simply using a simile to compare the woman he loves, at a key moment in their relationship, with a splendid mythological figure. His words do not touch upon the less attractive aspects of the Laodamia myth. *flagrans*, however, used by Catullus figuratively, but intelligible when taken literally, calls up those disturbing elements. The implications are obvious since it is Lesbia's excessive sexual appetite, about which Catullus rationalizes later in the poem (135 ff.), that threatens and ultimately destroys their relationship.

Line 75 adds another ominous note; the house to which Laodamia came was *incepta frustra*. Since lines 75-76 are grammatically connected with lines 73-74, the reader is invited to see in them a continuation of the simile. The Latin phrase is not simply equivalent to the Homeric ἡμιτελής; *frustra* carries with it a sense of anticipation, lack of fulfillment and disappointment. For the third time this seemingly innocent simile reveals a darker undercurrent. On one level, it is merely a Homeric simile. On another, however, it is still appropriate to Lesbia, who also is coming to a house *incepta frustra*. The relationship between her and Catullus could not be stabilized and formalized as a marriage, and therefore, as lines 135ff. reveal, it ultimately did not fulfil Catullus' expectations.

It is difficult to determine what the reader's expectations should be after line 76. If the idea that Protesilaus' death was divine retribution for neglect of a sacrifice[58] was widespread, the reader, not needing further elaboration, would probably have anticipated a return to Lesbia. If, however, this idea was not familiar or was invented by the poet (and for the modern reader these are the only possibilities), an expansion of it might be expected. Certainly the reader must feel that further information either about Laodamia, Lesbia, or both is required to explain fully the poet's choice of myth.[59] In any case, the long digression on Laodamia is extraordinary and surprising.

The apostrophe to Nemesis (77-78) signals clearly a movement away from Catullus' personal experience into the realm of mythological narrative:

> nil mihi tam valde placeat, Ramnusia virgo,
>   quod temere invitis suscipiatur eris.

The couplet is generally considered a serious prayer, apparently because up to this point Catullus has been speaking mainly of personal matters[60] and because otherwise the apostrophe seems incongruous. I would argue, however, that the poet expects the reader to recognize it as a common feature of mythological narrative. Direct address to a divinity or hero is used elsewhere in the Catullan corpus as it is in Greek, particularly Hellenistic, poetry. In the Attis poem (63), the apostrophe and prayer to the goddess (91-93) serve the same apotropaic function as here.[61] In poem 64 the poet invokes the heroes he intends to sing, particularly Peleus (22-30), and later addresses Ariadne (253). This device is apparently intended to enliven the narrative by bringing the narrator into the poem. For the same purpose the statement of a general truth may be inserted (e.g., *Ciris* 55: *nam verum fateamur: amat Polyhymnia verum.*), or self-apostrophe, as in Callim. *Aet.* 3 fr. 75.3-4 (Pf.):

> Ἥρην γάρ κοτέ φασι — κύον, κύον, ἴσχεο, λαιδρέ
>   θυμέ, σύ γ᾽ ἀείσῃ καὶ τά περ οὐχ ὁσίη·

Apollonius Rhodius expresses similar scruples about revealing what ought not be told concerning the secret rites of the island of Samothrace (*Argon.* 1.919-21):

> τῶν μὲν ἔτ᾽ οὐ προτέρω μυθήσομαι, ἀλλὰ καὶ αὐτή
> νῆσος ὁμῶς κεχάροιτο καὶ οἳ λάχον ὄργια κεῖνα
> δαίμονες ἐνναέται, τὰ μὲν οὐ θέμις ἄμμιν ἀείδειν·

In none of the examples cited above is the poet necessarily expressing his own opinion. It would be incredible to suggest that in poem 63 the poet has any genuine fear of falling victim to Cybele. Likewise, if Callimachus is reluctant to talk about embarrassing subjects, he could omit them completely without reproaching himself in mid-line. The poets' intrusions in all these cases are artificial but neither awkward nor disconcerting because the very nature of the subject matter has already required certain concessions on the part of the reader.

The apostrophe thus sets off the Laodamia passage from what has preceded it, as the poet represents Catullus' movement into another kind of poetry. The encomium, which has transformed into a love poem, now becomes a mythological narrative. The poet shows, however, that these changes are not easy or natural. In the midst of the Laodamia passage Catullus will remember his dead brother and repeat his lament for him (91-100), another demonstration that, in spite of Catullus' knowledge and use of poetic conventions, the grim realities of the world in which he lives interfere with the world he tries to create in verse.

Lines 79-86 elaborate on the subject of divine retribution and the intensity of Laodamia's passion:

> quam ieiuna pium desideret ara cruorem,
>   docta est amisso Laudamia viro,
> coniugis ante coacta novi dimittere collum,
>   quam veniens una atque altera rursus hiems
> noctibus in longis avidum saturasset amorem,
>   posset ut abrupto vivere coniugio,
> quod scibant Parcae non longo tempore abesse,
>   si miles muros isset ad Iliacos.

It is not clear whether the responsibility lies with Laodamia, with Protesilaus, or with both equally, but it is Laodamia who learns and who suffers the loss (*amisso viro*). The images of line 79, the thirsty altar and the blood, ironically called *pium*, seem particularly sinister.[62] Although these lines do not actually belong to the simile, the reader, aware of the original comparison between Lesbia and Laodamia, is invited to see here the implication that just as neglect of ritual was disastrous for Laodamia and Protesilaus, so too, the lack of ritual, the marriage ritual, was a fatal flaw in the relationship of Catullus and Lesbia. There may further be the implication that Lesbia bears the responsibility for the dissolution of their relationship because she has broken or did not properly complete the pledge that Catullus believes was made between them.[63]

The emphasis on passion in these lines is noteworthy. The separation of Laodamia from Protesilaus is the forced (*coacta*) loosening of her embrace from his neck. Her *avidus amor* remains unsatisfied. The nights that are denied are the long nights of winter. Line 84 conveys frustration; the idea is not that in a few years she would have become indifferent,[64] but that she had no memories at all of happiness to sustain her in her loneliness. From the revelations about Lesbia in the latter part of the poem it will become evident that she cannot be identified too closely with

the Laodamia of this passage. These lines, depicting Laodamia
desperately clinging to her mate and grieving at his departure, are
apparently wishful on Catullus' part, reflecting his illusions about how
Lesbia should feel and his insistence that she did once feel that way. The
desperate passion exhibited by Laodamia here, however, is more akin to
Catullus' own feelings about Lesbia, and hence these lines seem to serve
as a preparation for lines 105ff. where the point of comparison with
Laodamia shifts completely from Lesbia to Catullus.

The digression on Laodamia turns without change of tone to the
Trojan War. There is a grim artificiality of expression in the periphrasis
used for the summoning of the Greeks to Troy. Troy is a magnet, a siren
city (87-88):

> nam tum Helenae raptu primores Argivorum
>   coeperat ad sese Troia ciere viros,

With the introduction of Helen and the shift in focus from Laodamia and
Protesilaus to the Trojan War itself Catullus seems to have left the initial
comparison of Lesbia and Laodamia far behind and to have forgotten
completely his intention of writing about Allius. The digression, which
seems to remove the reader even farther from Catullus' personal experiences of the first seventy lines, makes the ensuing lament for the dead
brother all the more startling. With the mention of Helen, the poet also
raises the specter of adultery, implied in lines 67ff. and hinted at obliquely in line 73. Catullus will of course later in the poem admit openly that
his affair with Lesbia was adulterous.

The next couplet, an impassioned indictment of Troy, like the
apostrophe of Nemesis (77-78), constitutes a narrator's intrusion into his
poem (89-90):

> Troia (nefas!) commune sepulcrum Asiae Europaeque,
>   Troia virum et virtutum omnium acerba cinis,

The name of Troy did not have particularly terrible associations for the
Romans, but Catullus seems unable to mention it without violent reaction. At the very thought of the place, he launches into a lament for his
dead brother (91-100). The change of topics is abrupt, as Catullus
abandons the mythological past and without warning leaps into the real
present. The transition into the lament is made to seem even more
sudden by the use of a relative clause (91-96):[65]

> quaene etiam nostro letum miserabile fratri
>   attulit. ei misero frater adempte mihi,
> ei misero fratri iucundum lumen ademptum,
>   tecum una tota est nostra sepulta domus,
> omnia tecum una perierunt gaudia nostra,
>   quae tuus in vita dulcis alebat amor.

The statement made in the lament is perfectly intelligible, but its place and function in the poem are puzzling, as is the extensive repetition from the earlier lament (line 92 is almost identical to line 20 and 94-96 repeat 22-24 verbatim). At the very least the sudden intrusion into the mythological narrative of personal matters disrupts the flow of the poem, and it is disconcerting that what should be a passionate, almost involuntary outburst on Catullus' part is largely mere repetition of what we have already heard. These lines seem to lose their power the second time around.[66] Is the disconcerting effect of the second lament and particularly of the repeated lines calculated by the poet or merely an artistic failure?

In 68a the groundwork for the lament is well laid. As early as line 13 Catullus speaks of his own troubles (*accipe quis merser fortunae fluctibus ipse*). He proceeds with a brief description of the happy pursuits of his youth (15-18), contrasting them with his present troubles even before he has said what those troubles are. Line 19, introduced with the conjunction *sed*, marks a clear transition from past joy into present sorrow. Catullus' lament, an emotional outburst, when it occurs at this point, has a fine spontaneity, although it is not completely unexpected. In dramatic terms Catullus begins to explain his situation calmly but at the mention of his brother's death is overcome by a wave of anguish to which he gives expression. The transition back to Allius from the lament is likewise smooth. Lines 25-26 show Catullus regaining his composure and then resuming direct address to Allius. Thus the poet skillfully conveys Catullus' sorrow and despair and his struggle to come to grips with these emotions. The first lament is a logical outgrowth of the subject of the poem, as the second clearly is not. Here the sudden reversion from mythological narrative to personal matters is jarring. The transition from Troy to lament seems artificially contrived.

These observations, however, do not require us to excuse or permit us to dismiss lines 91-100.[67] The poet's intentions here are consistent with one of the determining themes of the poem, the conflict between the world the poet can create and shape to suit his fancy and the world in which he lives and over which he has little control. The lament occurring in a context ill-suited for it, awkwardly interrupting the mythological narrative, dramatizes Catullus' inability to insulate himself against unpleasantness simply by retreating into art. The sudden interjection of the lament, a deliberate reprise on the poet's part of the distress and isolation described in 68a, emphasizes the dichotomy between Catullus as poet and Catullus as a man who must daily face challenges and disappointments. The repetition of the same words and lines underscores the great difficulty of formulating any adequate response, let alone a poetic one, to an emotional crisis. One tends to say the same things over and over. The frailty of the medium of poetry is dramatized as the same thoughts, the same sense of loss, the same words, deeply moving in one context, sound inappropriate and formulaic in another. Catullus' personal crises have gained ascendancy to the point that they interfere with his control of his artistic medium. The poet has painted a dramatic picture of an artist whose troubled life is forcing itself into his works, even against his will, and yet whose creative endeavors are less and less able to give expression to these troubles. The same conflict will be in evidence again when the tensions caused by Lesbia's infidelity force themselves into Catullus' idealization of her (135ff.).

The lament contains two thematically important images. The light image, which will be resumed with Lesbia as *lux mea*, is introduced here for the first time and the *domus sepulta* reappears with new significance. *lumen* (93) is surely not the light of life taken from Catullus' brother (who would then be the *fratri* of that line). Given the repetition, *misero ... mihi, misero fratri*, it seems likely that the *lumen* is Catullus' brother, the *fratri* Catullus himself,[68] and that line 93 is a repetition of the idea expressed in line 92. This interpretation of *lumen* avoids an awkward change of addressees and, in view of what is said in the first lament of Catullus' relationship to his brother, the word is perfectly appropriate. The repetition of *iucundum* used earlier of the happy time of Catullus' youth, before his brother's death (*iucundum ver*, 16) supports this conclusion. Furthermore, if *lumen* refers to Catullus' brother, the two references to Lesbia as *lux mea* (132 and 160) gain in significance. One light has been taken from Catullus and the other, as becomes evident toward the end of the poem, is precariously close to being lost as well.

The first time the *domus sepulta* was mentioned it seemed to indicate simply that Catullus' family had suffered a serious loss. Now, however, three other *domus* have been introduced, the one Catullus insists is his proper house in Rome (32), the one Allius provided for Catullus and Lesbia, which is apparently the same house, and the house *incepta frustra* of Protesilaus and Laodamia, to which Allius' house is obliquely compared. The implication is that the death of the brother has, or should have, affected Catullus' relationship with Lesbia, or at least his perception of that relationship. I have noted above various indications that, although Catullus revolts against the idea, the poet regards the affair with Lesbia as a youthful escapade that has got out of hand. The buried *domus*, which Catullus uses in reference to his brother, but which has point in reference to Lesbia as well, seems to confirm this observation. At the conclusion of the poem, when Lesbia's infidelity and Catullus' desperate attempts at self-deception come into focus, it will be seen that just as the loss of *lux* is following fast upon the loss of *lumen*, so too the burial of the house of the rendezvous is imminent.

The lament concludes with a reminder that his brother died in a foreign land, far from home and family (97-100):

> quem nunc tam longe non inter nota sepulcra
> nec prope cognatos compositum cineres,
> sed Troia obscena, Troia infelice sepultum
> detinet extremo terra aliena solo.

The emphasis on its occurring so far away makes the death seem even more pathetic and conveys something of Catullus' feeling of helplessness. The curse placed on Troy (99-100) makes the transition back into mythological narrative smoother than that away from it was but underscores the artificiality of the lament in another way. The first time he curses Troy (89-90) Catullus speaks in the voice of narrator intruding himself into his mythological narrative; here, however, he is speaking in his own voice. The first curse is merely a stock poetic device, whereas the second is a personal and passionate, if illogical, expression of grief and frustration. By juxtaposing the two curses, similar in content but different in genesis, the poet again dramatically represents the tenuous line between the world of poetry and the world of reality. The next two couplets develop different aspects of the Trojan War and mark the return of Catullus to the role of narrator (101-104):

> ad quam tum properans fertur <lecta> undique pubes
> Graeca penetralis deseruisse focos,
> ne Paris abducta gavisus libera moecha
> otia pacato degeret in thalamo.

The first couplet emphasizes the tragedy of war. The Greeks leave the peace and security of their homes (*penetralis focos*) for the inhospitable plains of the Troad, where they will live for ten years in huts. The allusion to Protesilaus, who would have been one of the *pubes*, is unmistakable as *penetralis focos* echoes the *domum inceptam frustra* of lines 74-75. On another level, the couplet is an oblique allusion by the poet to Catullus' own situation. The act of leaving one's home to go to Troy calls to mind Catullus' brother who never returned from Troy and whose death there also resulted in the destruction of a house (*tota est nostra sepulta domus*, 22 and 94).

The next couplet places the Greeks' motive for attacking Troy in a cruel light. The focus changes from the tragedy of war to mean vindictiveness. The Greeks are not bent on recovering Helen but on denying pleasure to Paris. In line 87 Helen is described as the victim of *raptus* with no indication of her compliance. Here she is *abducta*, but she is also a *moecha*, an ugly word that for the Romans carried a burden of opprobrium. Thus the Troy passage ends on a bitter note. Laodamia's

widowhood is made to seem all the more pathetic by the suggestion that
Protesilaus lost his life in an enterprise supposedly heroic and romantic,
but which was actually motivated merely by revenge for a sordid crime.
The depiction of the Trojan War, then, is similar to the representation of
Allius' services and of Catullus' relationship to Lesbia; at the end of
each, the rose-colored spectacles are snatched away.

At line 105 Catullus returns to Laodamia with the vocative *pulcerrima
Laudamia*. From this point on, the comparison, entirely oblique, is between Laodamia and Catullus, not Lesbia.[69] Laodamia's emotions at the
loss and subsequent return of her husband are examined in a series of
three similes, the first of which is the longest and most complex (105-18):

> quo tibi tum casu, pulcerrima Laudamia,
>   ereptum est vita dulcius atque anima
> coniugium: tanto te absorbens vertice amoris
>   aestus in abruptum detulerat barathrum,
> quale ferunt Grai Pheneum prope Cyllenaeum
>   siccare emulsa pingue palude solum,
> quod quondam caesis montis fodisse medullis
>   audit falsiparens Amphitryoniades,
> tempore quo certa Stymphalia monstra sagitta
>   perculit imperio deterioris eri,
> pluribus ut caeli tereretur ianua divis,
>   Hebe nec longa virginitate foret,
> sed tuus altus amor barathro fuit altior illo,
>   qui tandem[70] indomitam ferre iugum docuit.

This simile is related to the earlier river simile (57-62). The studied
contrast between fresh mountain stream and swamp-draining *barathrum*,
the position of each simile in a set of three, and the fact that both describe
first an unpleasant thing, Catullus' tears and Laodamia's despair respectively, then a positive thing, Allius' aid and Laodamia's love at the
reunion, all indicate that the two similes should be considered together.
vertice (107) must mean pinnacle or height rather than whirlpool.[71] *vertice*
provides a contrast with *abruptum barathrum* and establishes a point of
reference for *altus amor* (117). Furthermore, height of love, that is, the
height of elation to which love raised Laodamia, is more intelligible than
whirlpool of love, which presumably would mean a confusion of emotions. *vertex* is used in the sense of pinnacle in the earlier river simile and,
if the manuscript reading *corruerit* (see above n. 35) is retained in line 52,
we have the additional link that both Laodamia and Catullus are cast
down in their desperation. Once the association of the two similes is
established, the reader is encouraged to seek similarities between
Catullus and Laodamia, and, as will be shown below, these abound.

The content and language of the simile are consistent with that of the preceding parts of the Laodamia passage. The *barathrum* simile, which itself becomes a digression on one of Hercules' accomplishments, has many of the characteristics of the compressed mythological narratives common in Hellenistic and neoteric poetry. It focuses on an obscure detail in the career of a familiar hero. Pausanias (8.14) is the only extant author directly to ascribe this work to Hercules.[72] Hercules' destruction of the Stymphalian birds, which is offered as the time of the creation of the channel, was traditionally the sixth labor and hence somewhat better known. The choice of words is in keeping with the spirit of Hellenistic poetry. *ferre* is used as it is in poem 64 (lines 19 and 212) to indicate that the poet is dealing with a traditional story. *audire* occurs in a non-Latin sense on analogy with the Greek ἀκούειν (112),[73] just as in poem 64 the word *nutrix* is used with the meaning "breast" on analogy with the Greek words for nurse and for breast, τιτθή and τιτθός.[74] Hercules is identified as *falsiparens Amphitryoniades* (112). The compound adjective, which occurs only here and may well be the poet's invention, is perhaps a rendering of Callimachus' ψευδοπάτωρ (*Cer.* 98), although Callimachus is expressing a different idea, and the patronymic was used by Hesiod and Theocritus.[75] It can be seen that in this short passage the poet is using with emphasis the stilted language of that type of poetry of which poem 64 is our best example in Latin. Catullus, leaving behind the lament that has intruded upon his narrative of Laodamia, returns to the poetic world with almost exaggeratedly appropriate language. When he attempts a similar escape from the realities of Lesbia's infidelity at line 138, however, his inability to do so will become painfully apparent.

Pervasive in the *barathrum* passage is the idea of death. Hercules dug this channel to drain flooding water from the Olbios River in Northeast Arcadia (Paus. 8.14), but certainly the best known river in this region was the River Styx. The word *barathrum* itself suggests the Underworld and at times has the meaning "death."[76] The depth of Laodamia's despair is linked with ideas of death, and the reader is induced to think of her impending suicide. On another level, there may be here an oblique allusion to Catullus' brother.

The digression on Hercules ends with a pair of periphrases that tell of his marriage to the goddess Hebe (115-16). The repetition of *tritum*, used of the threshold upon which Lesbia stepped as she entered the house (71), and the fact that Hercules too is presumably awaited by his beloved, serve to connect this passage with the earlier one. The reader is invited to compare and contrast the two scenes. Hercules and Hebe, like Laodamia and Protesilaus and unlike Catullus and Lesbia, enjoy legitimate marriage. Furthermore, while Hebe, like Laodamia (*indomitam* in line 118), comes to her marriage a virgin, Catullus' affair with Lesbia is frankly adulterous. Once again a common poetic device, this time periphrasis, when examined closely, betrays the conflicts at work here.

The next couplet brings the *barathrum* simile full cycle by introducing a second point of comparison (117-18). Now it serves to illustrate not the depth of Laodamia's despair but the depth of her love, which overcame death (*barathrum*) and finally taught her, a virgin (*indomitam*), to consummate the marriage. My emendation of *tuum domitum* to *tandem indomitam*[77] supports my position that from lines 117 on the subject is Laodamia's response to Protesilaus' return from the Underworld. Her deep love grows out of her deep despair, endures in the face of death, and is rewarded at last (*tandem*) with consummation that should have taken place on their wedding night. *ferre iugum* is a common figure for marriage or the loss of virginity,[78] and *indomitam* here must mean not "unbroken in spirit" but "virgin," the equivalent of ἀδμής.[79] The next two similes are more intelligible if taken as descriptions of her reaction to the reunion. It is hard to see why Protesilaus would be as dear as a long-despaired of heir, until he had himself been lost and despaired of. Furthermore, Laodamia did not have the opportunity to display dove-like faithfulness, nor, for that matter, dove-like passion, until her husband returned to her from the Underworld.

When the similes are viewed as describing Laodamia on Protesilaus' return, a number of similarities between the mythological heroine and Catullus himself arise. The only direct point of contact between Laodamia and Catullus is that both have lost loved ones at Troy, but there is a striking parallelism in their romantic experiences. Catullus' initial passion for Lesbia corresponds to Laodamia's passion at marriage. The former is thwarted by lack of a meeting place, the latter first by Protesilaus' departure and then by his death. Catullus' despair and frustration, reflected by his tears as described in the river simile, mirror Laodamia's emotions, described in the *barathrum*-simile. Both similes end, however, in fulfillment. Catullus' meeting with Lesbia at the house Allius provided corresponds to Laodamia's reunion with Protesilaus. Both are periods of longed for and despaired of joy and passion. In poem 68 the Laodamia passage ends with the reunion, but the informed reader is well aware that Protesilaus' return is only for a short time and that his second departure will throw Laodamia into such a paroxysm of grief that she will commit suicide. After Catullus has revealed Lesbia's infidelity and made his unconvincing resolutions of tolerance, it becomes apparent that his joy too has been short-lived. Like Laodamia, he only temporarily overcomes his unhappiness, and in the end the result seems to be worse than if he had never had that brief moment of fulfillment.

The next two similes develop various aspects of Laodamia's and, by implication, Catullus' love (119-30):

nam nec tam carum confecto aetate parenti
    una caput seri nata nepotis alit,
qui, cum divitiis vix tandem inventus avitis
    nomen testatas intulit in tabulas,
impia derisi gentilis gaudia tollens
    suscitat a cano volturium capiti:
nec tantum niveo gavisa est ulla columbo
    compar, quae multo dicitur improbius
oscula mordenti semper decerpere rostro,
    quam quae praecipue multivola est mulier.
sed tu horum magnos vicisti sola furores,
    ut semel es flavo conciliata viro.

The first simile is one of the few imitations of Pindar in the Catullan corpus.[80] In Pindar (*Ol.* 10.86ff.) a father himself rejoices in his heir and no *gentilis* is introduced as unworthy recipient of another's wealth. The actual points of comparison are the chagrin at seeing what one has accumulated pass out of the family and the disappointment of having good deeds pass unrecorded. He who has a poet to sing his praises is fortunate, as is the man with an heir. The borrowing from Pindar may then be an oblique reminder that 68b began as an endeavor on Catullus' part to commemorate Allius' good services to him.

The main function of the simile, however, is to describe Laodamia's joy at Protesilaus' return from the Underworld, likening it to the thrill the old man feels at the unexpected arrival of a new life and reprieve. There is no *quam* corresponding to the *tam* of line 119, and presumably the reader is to supply *quam Protesilaum tibi reductum* or the like. The simile operates on more than one level, for a grandfather's relationship with his grandson is not the same as a wife's relationship with her husband. Laodamia was first introduced with emphasis on physical passion (*flagrans amore*) and this was her outstanding characteristic in the ancient tradition, but here her love for Protesilaus is given a spiritual quality as well. There is, however, cruel irony in the image of the grandfather and child. In spite of the brief reunion, Laodamia will not live long enough to give birth to a child. In having Catullus expand the simile beyond the requirements of the context and emphasize inheritance and continuation of the family, the poet hints at a certain wishfulness on Catullus' part. The relationship with Lesbia does not even achieve permanence, let alone lead to marriage and family as Catullus' language here, and more pointedly at lines 143-46, indicates that he desired.

The third simile (125-30) returns to Laodamia's sexual passion but also underscores her faithfulness. The dove was a well-known symbol of faithfulness,[81] but here her passion is emphasized (*multo improbius*; *oscula mordenti semper decerpere rostro*; *multivola*). Here is expressed Catullus' ideal love, a combination of intense physical passion and deep spiritual unity and constancy. Laodamia attained this ideal, although, as *semel* ominously reminds us, only briefly. Catullus seems to feel that he too was capable of and succeeded in achieving it, although in his case too it lasted only a short time.

The merging and separating of these two aspects of love are of central importance to a number of the Lesbia epigrams, most notably poem 72:

> dicebas quondam solum te nosse Catullum,
>   Lesbia, nec prae me velle tenere Iovem.
> dilexi tum te non tantum ut vulgus amicam,
>   sed pater ut gnatos diligit et generos.
> nunc te cognovi: quare, etsi impensius uror,
>   multo mi tamen es vilior et levior.
> qui potis est, inquis? quod amantem iniuria talis
>   cogit amare magis, sed bene velle minus.

Underlying the characterization here of a Laodamia who combines both *amare* and *diligere* in her relations with Protesilaus is our awareness that Catullus sought just such a relationship and that the Lesbia of the Catullan corpus, and as we will soon discover, particularly the Lesbia of poem 68, either would not or could not achieve this combination.

Protesilaus' return brings Catullus' thoughts back to his own beloved, and finally he resumes his description of Lesbia entering the house (131-34):

> aut nihil aut paulo[82] cui tum concedere digna
>   lux mea se nostrum contulit in gremium,
> quam circumcursans hinc illinc saepe Cupido
>   fulgebat crocina candidus in tunica.

The antecedent of *cui* is generally considered to be Laodamia, but a strong case can be made for seeing here a comparison between Lesbia and Protesilaus. Throughout the second half of the Laodamia passage (105-30), the implied comparison has been between the mythological heroine and Catullus, not Lesbia. At the time of the reunion, as opposed to the time of the marriage, it is Protesilaus who approaches the waiting Laodamia, as Lesbia approaches the waiting Catullus. The parallels between Catullus and Laodamia I have noted above point to a most important similarity between Protesilaus and Lesbia. Both come to their lovers for brief periods of intense love and joy, but are also soon to depart, Protesilaus permanently back to the Underworld, Lesbia occasionally to her *furta* (137). The qualification *aut nihil aut paulo*, which has troubled many,[83] is now easily explained. Lesbia did stay longer than the three hours or single day allotted to Protesilaus, although to Catullus the period of time was still relatively and unbearably brief.

At line 132 Lesbia, as she advances to Catullus' embrace, is called *lux mea*. The expression may be colloquial[84] but the image is thematically important. If Catullus' brother is the *lumen* of line 93, then Lesbia is here linked with him. We already know that Catullus has lost his brother irrevocably, and we shall soon see how close he is to losing Lesbia as well. The repetition of *lux mea* in the last line of the poem in conjunction with *vivere* and *viva* (adjective) will underscore Catullus' despair at the prospect of losing his *lux* as he has lost his *lumen*.

At line 133 Catullus launches into a flight of fancy. Cupid, bright and conspicuous in his saffron tunic, attends Lesbia, dancing about her. The language here recalls Lesbia's entrance (70-72) (*fulgebat/fulgentem plantam*; *candidus/candida diva*).[85] Cupid, dressed as the wedding god Hymen would be, seems to act as surrogate for that divinity. Thus the reader is again reminded that although Catullus and Lesbia are not husband and wife, Catullus seems to regard their relationship as symbolically equivalent to marriage.

The image of the god accompanying the mortal woman is a bit extravagant. There is no simile here; Catullus says that Cupid was actually there with Lesbia. He seems so caught up in his fevered reminiscence as to have lost all perspective. This whimsical indulgence, however, is followed in line 135 with the admission of his knowledge of Lesbia's infidelity. The sharp contrast between that revelation and the extraordinary image of Cupid heightens the shock of line 135.

The next three lines, in violent conflict with all Catullus has said about Lesbia up to this point (but for which the poet, operating on a more informed level, has laid the groundwork), are dismaying and devastating (135-37):

> quae tamen etsi uno non est contenta Catullo,
>   rara verecundae furta feremus erae,
> ne nimium simus stultorum more molesti.

The woman Catullus has deified, whose rendezvous with him was so glorious, is suddenly revealed as worse than faithless. She is not satisfied with Catullus alone but has another lover or lovers besides. *contenta* shows without question that the complaint is not about Lesbia's husband but about another man or men.[86] Even more confusing than the revelation of Lesbia's infidelity, however, is Catullus' resolution to endure it. Lines 135-37 cancel out virtually everything Catullus has said up to this point and force the reader to ask how Catullus could at the same time be passionately idealistic and coldly indifferent. Such a dichotomy is simply not possible.

The distinction I have maintained between the poet and Catullus allows a resolution of this paradox. Catullus is engaged in gross self-deception, and the poet intentionally makes his resolution of sophisticated indifference sound unconvincing and pathetic. Catullus apparently seeks a wry effect in referring to himself by name,[87] but the verb *feremus* constitutes a tacit admission that Lesbia's *furta* are in fact distressing. He attempts to justify and to rationalize his attitude by noting the infrequency of her betrayals, but his words ring false. The outrageous inappropriateness of *verecundae* exposes his self-deception and self-contradiction.[88] Only to an extremely confused or desperate mind can the Lesbia of lines 135ff. be called *verecunda*. The poet depicts Catullus striving to believe that Lesbia is still his, insisting she is *verecunda* when in fact the best he can hope for is that he be spared knowledge of her other affairs. *erae* (136) is most revealing. It will not do to regard the word as a synonym for *domina* (even if one takes the *domina* of lines 68 and 156 to be Lesbia). *era* seems always to have been a stronger word with more precise uses and generally applied to owners of slaves and to goddesses (*ThLL* V 2, 850), and whereas *domina* came to be used commonly in love elegy for the beloved woman, *era* is never so used.[89] Since Lesbia has been represented as a goddess (70), *era* might be an extension of the idea. Or the poet could be casting Catullus in the role of Lesbia's slave. In either case the relationship is that of an inferior to one who has absolute power over him. The casual attitude Catullus has assumed is exposed as a facade. He endures Lesbia's infidelities because he feels he has no other option. By careful use of vocabulary the poet shows that Catullus does not have the confidence he makes a show of, but rather is trying to convince himself that his situation is not as hopeless as it really is. The unpleasant realities of Catullus' life have again intruded on his poetic endeavors, leaving in a shambles his encomium of his beloved and the glowing description of his romance.

At line 138 Catullus returns or perhaps retreats to mythology (138-40):

> saepe etiam Iuno, maxima caelicolum,
> coniugis in culpa flagrantem concoquit iram,
> noscens omnivoli plurima furta Iovis.

The abrupt transition in the middle of the distich calls special attention to this movement from actuality back to the world of imagination and myth. The echoes in line 139 of line 73 (*coniugis/coniugis; flagrantem/flagrans*), emphasize the drastic change that has taken place. The first time Catullus invoked a mythological figure it was to describe a glorious moment of love and happiness. Here he invokes one to justify cynical nonchalance in the face of betrayal. The shift from idealization to harsh reality and back to mythological exemplum dramatizes Catullus' struggle. Just as the devastating loss of his brother intruded into the Laodamia passage in the form of a lament (91-100), so here the awareness of the deteriorating relationship with Lesbia intrudes upon his glorification of her. His attempts to mold reality by selective description and poetic manipulation are failing in the face of overwhelming difficulties and disappointments.

On the surface, Catullus merely uses the common device of a mythological exemplum to support the position he has taken in lines 135-37. If Juno, who could not remain ignorant of Jupiter's frequent indiscretions, manages to control her temper, surely Catullus can put up with Lesbia's occasional lapses. On another level, however, the example the poet chooses and the words with which he presents it reinforce the sense of Catullus' submissiveness and helplessness. However one emends line 139,[90] it seems clear that Juno is outraged and that an effort is required on her part to keep her anger in check. No explanation for her restraint is offered. She is called *maxima caelicolum*, and of her sex she is supreme. Her authority, however, does not extend over Jupiter who is capable of bullying her (e.g., Hom. *Il.* 1.561-67). Moreover the linking of Catullus and Juno results in an implied connection of Lesbia and Jupiter, who is *omnivolus* and who does wrong (*culpa*) by committing *furta*. Thus the blame Catullus dares not place directly on Lesbia is implied obliquely. In having Catullus offer Juno as a model for his attitude, the poet indicates that Lesbia's conduct actually does cause Catullus anger and pain and that he does consider her guilty in her infidelity, stifling his anger not out of sophisticated nonchalance, but rather, like Juno, out of fear of the consequences of a confrontation.

Line 141 seems a sententious statement: *atqui nec divis homines componier aequum est.* The point may be that if a divinity like Juno tolerates infidelity then a mere mortal like Catullus ought not presume to do otherwise. Another possibility is that the line is the beginning of an examination of Catullus' status in relation to his own *diva*, Lesbia, although this seems too self-effacing even for the Catullus of the last part of the poem. Interpretation of the line is rendered more difficult because there is almost certainly a lacuna of at least one couplet between lines 141 and 142.[91] Line 142, *ingratum tremuli tolle parentis onus*, does not follow smoothly upon line 141. Such an abrupt transition to self-apostrophe, with no vocative or other indication of the change, would be awkward, and the meaning of the line, "Away with the thankless burden of a doddering parent," is certainly not clear in its position immediately after line 141. Most likely line 141 was followed by a brief restatement of the resolve to be tolerant of Lesbia's behavior; then immediately before line 142 the observation would have been made that after all Lesbia is a grown woman and

Catullus is not her father. Perhaps there was a vocative in this line or couplet. Then line 142 could be read as an emotional outburst by Catullus in which he orders himself indirectly to stop worrying about that which he is not in a position to control and for which he is not responsible anyway.

Catullus adds a third justification for the casual indifference he has attempted to assume (143-46):

> nec tamen illa mihi dextra deducta paterna
>   fragrantem Assyrio venit odore domum,
> sed furtiva dedit mira munuscula nocte,
>   ipsius ex ipso dempta viri gremio.

Since he is not her husband he has no real claim on her; she was in fact married to another and came to Catullus secretly. The two images describing the circumstances of legitimate marriage are agreeable, even pleasant. The first apparently refers to preparation of the marriage contract deposited at a temple on the day of the wedding. The mention of the bride's father brings to mind ideas of continuity of the family line and of the solemnity of the rituals. The second image, the house scented with Oriental incense, appeals directly to the senses. The subject here, however, is what did not happen. The poet has thus injected more than a touch of wistfulness into Catullus' description of the marriage that never took place and the house that he and Lesbia did not share. Furthermore, the ideas of house and marriage call to mind Lesbia's first entrance to the house and her ill-omened act of stepping on the threshold.

If the marriage that did not take place is presented as an agreeable fantasy, the account of what actually did occur is couched in terms that are ambivalent. Instead of marriage, Catullus got *furtiva munuscula. furtiva* picks up on the two occurrences of *furta* earlier (Lesbia's at line 136 and Jupiter's at line 140). Thus Lesbia's relationship with Catullus is likened to her affairs with other men, another one of her escapades. *munuscula* is hard to assess. The diminutive may show affection and be colloquial (*ThLL* VIII 1667-68), but there is no other example of the word used specifically as a euphemism for a woman's favors. It seems not to be entirely innocent here; the *communes amores* of line 69 have been reduced to duties owed to a husband but purloined (*dempta*) for Catullus. The act of adultery is emphasized by the two intensives (*ipsius, ipso,* 146). This does not seem to be boasting on Catullus' part. Rather there is regret in this final and violent admission that his affair was a furtive adventure, not a grand encounter. The only positive phrase in this couplet is *mira nocte,*[92] which serves, as did his detailed reminiscence in lines 70-72 to emphasize the importance, in spite of everything that has happened since, that this meeting had for him.

The next couplet contains Catullus' final concession (147-48):

> quare illud satis est, si nobis is datur unis
> quem lapide illa diem[93] candidiore notat.

Catullus will be satisfied if Lesbia cherishes those days she does spend with him. This sentiment, expressed as the homely practice of marking good and bad days with white and black stones respectively,[94] is an abrupt and disappointing conclusion to this section of the poem. That he may merely be her favorite among many is hardly a worthy aspiration for any man, let alone one as single minded as Catullus has shown himself everywhere else in the Lesbia poems and especially in 68b. To make matters worse, there is no guarantee that Lesbia will concede even the little Catullus asks. It will be enough for him, he says, if she does so.

This conclusion, so strikingly anticlimactic, underscores powerfully the discrepancy between the lofty assertions Catullus has made about Lesbia and the hard, unpleasant realities of the relationship. On another level, the words expose Catullus' vulnerability as well as his profound unhappiness with the situation. By juxtaposition of the revelation of the true state of affairs with the idealization of Lesbia, the poet dramatizes Catullus' struggle to force into existence the reciprocation his own commitment demands. At play throughout this section of the poem is the conflict between a poet's ability to conjure up at will images such as that of a Cupid or a *candida diva*, to create for himself an ideal world, and his inability to control or soften the blows of reality, the death of a brother or the unfaithfulness of a mistress. And as this section of the poem closes, harsh reality is in the ascendant to the point that it even undermines Catullus' attempt to flee from it into his art.

The poem concludes with an epilogue (68c, 149-60) set off from 68b by a sharp break, just as 68b is set off from 68a. At line 41, the invocation of the Muses clearly demands a change in voice, marking the beginning of the tribute to Allius, a unit of the poem related to but distinct from the epistle of the first forty lines. Similarly the return to direct address indicated by *tibi* (149) and the vocative *Alli* (150), which must be the correct reading here, shows that the tribute, such as it is, has been completed (149-50):

> hoc tibi, quod potui, confectum carmine munus
> pro multis, Alli, redditur officiis,

The epilogue begins with an apology. Catullus qualifies his offering of a *confectum carmine munus* with the parenthetic *quod potui. munus* echoes the two previous mentions of the *munera* (10, 32) which Catullus was unable to provide. *quod potui* seems to acknowledge that Catullus is not able to come to Allius as requested and that the poem is not what Allius is

expecting. It may further be Catullus' admission that his intentions of
praising Allius have been side-tracked by the thoughts of Lesbia and of
his brother's death. *multis officiis* recalls the *officium* about which Catullus
declared he could not keep silent (4) and the *hospitis officium* (12) owed to
Allius. The reader now understands that Allius' *officium* was to make the
house available to Catullus and Lesbia. The next couplet repeats the concern expressed at the start of 68b (41-50) that Allius' good services and
name not pass into oblivion (151-52):

> ne vestrum scabra tangat robigine nomen
> haec atque illa dies atque alia atque alia.

The image of time as destroyer of the memory of human actions is reintroduced here as Allius' name must be protected from *scabra robigine*.
Earlier Catullus expressed a similar wish of keeping his friend's *studium*
from being covered by *caeca nocte* (43-44) and his name by the spider's
web (49-50). The elisions and repetitions in line 152 give a sense of con-
tinuous passage of time much as the repetition in line 47 (*notescatque magis
mortuus atque magis*) does. These unmistakable echoes remind the reader
that the stated purpose of 68b was to commemorate Allius, who has been
overshadowed and all but forgotten since Lesbia's entrance into the
poem.

The next couplet expresses the hope that the gods will add their own
gifts to Catullus' (153-54):

> huc addent divi quam plurima, quae Themis olim
> antiquis solita est munera ferre piis.

This allusion to the age of heroes[95] serves two functions. First, insofar as
the epilogue is a recapitulation of the earlier parts of the poem, this
couplet provides a point of contact with the mythological sections of the
poem, the story of Laodamia and Protesilaus and the account of
Hercules, a hero who himself received reward from the gods. Second, it
reaffirms that Catullus still regards Allius' service to him as an act of
pietas, worthy of commemoration. When at line 68, after a dramatic and
elaborate introduction, the true nature of Allius' service was first revealed, the reader felt that Catullus was attempting to ennoble an act
which in fact merely reflected a willingness to help a friend in a rather
tawdry situation. Now, in light of what has been learned about Lesbia,
this feeling has been reinforced. Catullus' insistence on the need to immortalize Allius' services seems to reflect his own need to avoid admitting
that the affair with Lesbia is not permanent, that it has almost run its
course. It is as if he feels that by keeping alive the memory of the house
Allius provided, he can keep alive as well the affair that began there.

The poem concludes with a benediction on a catalogue of the people who have appeared elsewhere in the poem (155-60):

> sitis felices et tu simul et tua vita,
>   et domus < ipsa > [96] in qua lusimus, et domina,
> et qui principio nobis †terram dedit aufert†,
>   a quo sunt primo omnia nata bona,
> et longe ante omnes mihi quae me carior ipso est,
>   lux mea, qua viva vivere dulce mihi est.

Catullus first wishes happiness to Allius and his beloved.[97] The mention of the woman is a surprise since she appears only by implication earlier in the poem. This unambiguous reference to Allius' beloved should serve as supporting evidence for the poem's unity and indicate that Allius' misfortune, as set forth at the beginning of the poem, involves only a temporary separation from and certainly not the death of his beloved. That Allius' *vita* should be included in the benediction also seems to confirm Allius' condition in the first eight lines as not entirely desperate but exaggerated in the elaborate imagery used to describe it.

In the next line the good wishes are extended to the house itself in which Catullus and Lesbia met and to the mistress of the house.[98] *domina* here is not a subject of *lusimus* but, like *domus*, of the implied *sit felix. in qua lusimus* calls to mind line 17 (*multa satis lusi*) where Catullus contrasts the happy life he led prior to his brother's death with his present melancholy condition. This allusion to the earlier passage emphasizes that the house of the rendezvous belongs to a past which, although probably not chronologically distant, is far removed from the present as far as Catullus' state of mind is concerned. The use of *lusimus* again links the Lesbia affair with the youthful adventures, which now, in light of his brother's death, Catullus considers to have been frivolous. The poem ends with a declaration of Catullus' confirmed devotion to Lesbia. Here, however, just before that conclusion, the poet reinforces the idea that Catullus has begun to recognize the truth about his love affair—that it is not the permanent and serious relationship he had envisioned but merely another youthful escapade that has got out of hand. Catullus is not ready to admit that his affair with Lesbia has collapsed, but by the end of poem 68 the poet has made the reader well aware of it.

The next couplet, hopelessly corrupt, ought, it seems, to refer to Catullus' brother.[99] Introduction of a new person into the poem at this point would be awkward and inartistic, and Catullus' brother is the only person who has appeared in the poem and is not mentioned otherwise in the benediction. A reference to the dead amid a benediction to the living is admittedly odd, but throughout poem 68 there appear disturbing and surprising elements which often seem incongruous in their immediate context. The second lament for the dead brother, interrupting the Laodamia passage, and the sudden revelation of Lesbia's infidelity are the two most striking examples. Lines 157-58 might then constitute another and the final demonstration that Catullus cannot escape the haunting sorrow he feels at the loss of his brother; here again the poet makes the sorrow intrude on Catullus' thoughts at a moment when it seems inappropriate for him to do so. Furthermore a reference to the dead brother following upon the word *lusimus* (156) would reinforce the contrast between the youthful joys of the past and the deep sorrow of the present.

The final couplet belongs to Lesbia. Catullus places her above all others; she is dearer to him than he is to himself, and as long as she is alive living is sweet for him. These sentiments would have caused no surprise after the first introduction of Lesbia, but how are they to be understood in light of her infidelity and Catullus' self-abasement (135-48)? Key phrases seem to be *lux mea* and *qua viva*. In the second lament Catullus' brother was called *lumen* (93), and both laments testify to the important place he occupied in Catullus' life. Lesbia here is called *lux* for the second time (*lux mea*, 132), and that she is living is strongly emphasized. Catullus here seems to declare his intention of cherishing what little he still has for as long as he can hold it. He wishes desperately to keep Lesbia, the most important thing in his life, even at the cost of the pain of betrayal and the constant need to deceive himself. In 68b, however, especially in lines 135-48, the poet has dramatically represented the strain Catullus is under, and considering this, the reader must suspect that even in this resolve Catullus is engaging in self-deception.

CONCLUSION

The analysis presented here has, I believe, demonstrated that poem 68 is a unified whole, carefully conceived and executed. Little, if anything, is extraneous; every passage, every image has been conceived with an eye to its effectiveness in delineating the major themes of the poem. According to the interpretation offered here, these are two: a putting into perspective of the relationship with Lesbia and an exploration of the conflict between the world a poet can create in his art and the world in which he must live.

The latter is dramatized in two ways. First, people and events are presented in elevated and richly figured language only to be shown to be, in actuality, pedestrian or even sordid, clear examples of a poet's making assertions that are not supported by the facts. Second, Catullus, who is depicted as the composer first of a verse epistle, then of an encomium, seems at times to let the pressures of his life, his brother's death and Lesbia's infidelity, intrude upon his poetry, interrupting the flow of 68b and confronting the reader with incongruities.

In setting forth Allius' misfortune in his love affair, Catullus uses simile and metaphor, making the plight of this typical lover sound almost tragic. When he turns to speak of his own loss, the more serious and irreparable loss of his brother, his language is much plainer, direct and unadorned. Thus while Allius' trifling distress is a subject for poetic elaboration, in a real crisis a poet finds little to say. After seeming to conclude that he cannot help Allius because of his own troubles, Catullus launches on an encomium. Suddenly he has again at his disposal all the devices of the poetic art which had failed him when speaking of his brother. Invoking the Muses, he begins to pile image upon image. He first proclaims his intention of immortalizing Allius, then embellishes in a series of similes the anguish he himself suffered and the salvation Allius brought him. In describing his sorrow in love, Catullus does not show the lack of inspiration he has claimed was caused by the death of his brother. After the long and elaborate build-up, Allius' service is revealed in two lines, and proves to have been relatively slight, the sort of thing one ought not to publicize, and it becomes clear that Catullus' lofty language cannot really ennoble Allius' service in adultery. Lesbia is introduced with sharp, striking imagery, raised to the rank of a goddess with Cupid himself in her retinue. Eventually, however, the realities of Lesbia's attitude intrude upon the idealization. Catullus' lofty assertions do not allow him to ignore his predicament. The attitude Catullus assumes of tolerating her infidelity and being thankful for the days she spends with him is at best cynical, at worst pathetic, and in either case completely at odds with the idealized picture that has preceded it. The poet here represents Catullus molding in verse the world as he wishes it to be and the love affair he would like, but the flawed love affair with the real Lesbia interrupts this reverie, as the harsh realities of his life afflict even his ability to compose poetry.

The same sort of disruption is in evidence in the second lament for his dead brother. At the point at which it occurs the poem has moved into the sphere of mythological narrative, and Catullus has assumed the role of narrator. At the mention of Troy, however, the illusion is shattered and he returns suddenly to his personal situation. Again we see the exigencies of the world in which the poet lives intruding upon the world he can create in his verse. The repetition of lines from the first lament further dramatizes the inadequacy for Catullus of poetic response to true crisis. Catullus has found numerous ways to express his distress in love and will soon display similar dexterity in describing Laodamia's reaction to her loss, but in responding to the death of his brother he can only repeat what he has said before. To underscore further the dichotomy between the two worlds, when Catullus returns again to the mythological narrative, the poet has him do so with emphatic use of the vocabulary and mannerisms of epic and epyllion.

The second major concern of poem 68, the relation of Catullus with Lesbia, is closely tied to the first. Much of what is said on this matter operates on two levels. On one, Catullus speaks. He tells of his distress in elaborate similes, recalling in minute detail the approach of Lesbia, whom he calls a goddess and compares to a mythological heroine. He admits she is not faithful to him but resolves to be tolerant calling her *verecunda* in spite of her *furta*. He then goes on to provide various justifications and explanations of his attitude. On this level, the incongruity between Catullus' idealization of Lesbia and his acknowledgment of the true situation reflect the dichotomy between poetic representation and actuality.

On another level, that is, on the level at which the poet is operating, there are indications that Catullus' relationship with Lesbia is unsatisfactory, that it may, in fact, be disintegrating completely. The first hint of this comes when Catullus' distress is linked by language with Allius' and thus contrasted with Catullus' sorrow over the loss of his brother. The implication is that, whether Catullus realizes it or not, his affair with Lesbia should be considered just another of his youthful *lusus* and should, with the rest of them, be laid to rest. Next, as Lesbia enters the house, the detail of her ill-omened act of stepping on the threshold is emphasized.

The comparison with Laodamia is worded to indicate that Lesbia was married to another, that she was driven more by lust than by love, and that the house in which she and Catullus met ultimately held disappointment and sorrow. The recurrent images contained in the river and *barathrum* similes link Catullus with Laodamia and Lesbia with Protesilaus, thus forecasting an unhappy ending to Catullus' love affair. Catullus' resolution to be tolerant is cast into language that makes him sound subservient and intimidated. The example of Jupiter and Juno depicts just such a situation. The observation that Lesbia is not his wife is so worded as to indicate that Catullus would have much preferred legitimate marriage to the relationship he actually did have. The last line of the poem, connecting Lesbia (*lux mea*) with Catullus' lost brother (*lumen*) constitutes the final and desperate assertion of a confused and vulnerable man, clinging to what little he has left. The poet, operating on a more informed level, shows that the relationship with Lesbia is all but over and that all that survive are Catullus' insistence that it is not and the poetic embellishments with which he tries to avoid facing the truth.

Thus the poem that represents the beginning of the genre of Latin love elegy is also the culmination of the poetry of the Catullan corpus. Regardless of where poem 68 stands chronologically and in relation to poem 64, it must be viewed as the poet's most important poem, in that it constitutes his fullest and most probing examination both of the major theme of his poetry, namely his love for Lesbia, and of his position in the world as a creative artist.

APPENDIX: THE LAODAMIA MYTH

Most of the testimony we have on the Laodamia myth is from relative-ly late sources. While we know of treatments that predate poem 68, it is not possible to establish in any detail which versions of the myth these represented. Homer (*Il.* 2.698-701) gives no details beyond Protesilaus' death and does not even name the widow, describing her only as ἀμφιδρυφής. According to Pausanias (4.2.7), Protesilaus' wife was called Polydora in the *Cypria*. Pausanias says that in this poem the widow took her own life but does not make it clear whether this act followed Pro-tesilaus' death or his return to the Underworld after the reunion. The word Pausanias uses of her suicide, ἐπικατασφάζειν, "to slay over or in succession to a corpse," makes it unlikely that the *Cypria* dealt with the version in which she dies following the image of her husband into the fire.

The few surviving fragments from Euripides' tragedy *Protesilaus*, of uncertain date, do little to shed light on the episodes and incidents of the play. According to the brief synopsis of the play that has been preserved (*Schol. Aristid.* p. 671), Protesilaus left Laodamia on their wedding day. After his death he obtained permission to return to his wife for a single day. The synopsis makes no mention of Laodamia's suicide or of the image. One fragment is especially tantalizing (fr. 655, Nauck²): οὐκ ἂν προδοίην καίπερ ἄψυχον φίλον. If ἄψυχον means "inanimate" here, it could be a reference to the image that Laodamia made. If, however, it simply means "lifeless," i.e., "dead," the line could belong to her refusal of her father's request that she remarry.

The next treatment of the myth of which we have knowledge is the *Pro-tesilaodamia* of Laevius (born ca. 129 B.C.). The surviving fragments do not allow anything approaching a complete reconstruction of the poem,[1] but there seem to have been a wedding scene and a lament by Laodamia addressed to the absent Protesilaus. Laevius may have offered a full and detailed treatment of the myth, but the lack of proportion in many Hellenistic and Latin narrative poems and the fondness for emphasizing one aspect of the myth at the expense of others forbid our taking such a full account for granted. It is nevertheless noteworthy that a Roman poet handled the myth of Laodamia and Protesilaus comparatively close to the composition of poem 68.

There is no record of any Hellenistic poem devoted to this myth.[2] From the type of stories collected in Parthenius' *Erotica Pathemata* it can be seen that the main features of the story, Protesilaus' return from the dead, Laodamia's suicide, and the image with which she had intercourse, would have appealed to the imagination of the poets of the Hellenistic period.[3] Nevertheless we cannot postulate a Hellenistic model for the Laodamia passage in poem 68, and it is unlikely anyway that in a poem so highly original the poet is adhering to any single account to the point of direct imitation. Euripides and Laevius were probably the main sources.

To what extent would readers of poem 68 have known the range of variations in the Laodamia myth? From Euripides they would probably have known of Protesilaus' return from the dead. Some, perhaps most, would have known the account of the *Cypria*, in which the widow commits suicide. Would they have been familiar with the version in which Laodamia constructs an image of her dead husband and ends her life by pursuing it into the fire? Here Ovid is of assistance. In two passages there are indications that he expected his readers to know this version of the story. In one, Laodamia writes to Protesilaus at some time after his departure for Troy (*Her.* 13.149-57):

> dum tamen arma geres diverso miles in orbe,
>   quae referat vultus est mihi cera tuos:
> illi blanditias, illi tibi debita verba
>   dicimus, amplexus accipit illa meos.
> crede mihi, plus est, quam quod videatur, imago;
>   adde sonum cerae, Protesilaus erit.
> hanc specto teneoque sinu pro coniuge vero
>   et tamquam possit verba referre, queror.

In the second passage Ovid uses Laodamia as a negative example (*Rem. Am.* 715-24):

> exiguum est, quod deinde canam, sed profuit illud
>   exiguum multis, in quibus ipse fui.
> scripta cave relegas blandae servata puellae:
>   constantis animos scripta relecta movent.
> omnia pone feros (pones invitus) in ignes
>   et dic 'ardoris sit rogus iste mei.'
> Thestias absentem succendit stipite natum:
>   tu timide flammae perfida verba dabis?
> si potes, et ceras remove: quid imagine muta
>   carperis? hoc periit Laodamia modo.

Knowledge of the story of Laodamia and the image is essential to full appreciation of Ovid's irony in these passages. In the first Laodamia's words taken at face value seem extravagant but innocent enough. They are much more humorous and ironic to the reader who is aware that she is obtaining sexual gratification from the image. Ovid seems to be the only author to place the building of the image in Protesilaus' lifetime, a change perhaps resulting from his desire to present this important element of the myth within the confines of the epistolary format of the

Heroides.[4] In the second passage, where Ovid seems to follow the traditional sequence of events, Laodamia is linked with the idea of wax images. Ovid advises that one destroy old love letters and images of former lovers. The words one should speak when burning these remembrances, *ardoris sit rogus iste mei*, could well serve as Laodamia's final utterance. The fire in which her father disposes of the image becomes the pyre of her passion as well. There is irony in the question *quid imagine muta carperis*, for Laodamia certainly found use for her *imago muta*, and there is a *double-entendre* in the verb *periit*. These lines offer so much more in overtones and irony to one fully apprised of the image version of the myth that it seems certain that Ovid's readers were familiar with that variation. Since there is no evidence for a detailed treatment of the poem in the interval, we must assume that the readers of poem 68 also knew this version of the story. Indeed although neither Laodamia's suicide nor the image are mentioned explicitly in 68, the phrase *flagrans amore* with which she is introduced obliquely hints at both.

Poem 68 seems to introduce one new element to the traditional accounts, neglect of the gods as responsible for Protesilaus' death. The only reference to the idea of divine retribution occurs in Eust. *Il.* 325, but the vague terms he uses, χολῷ 'Αφροδίτης and μῆνιν 'Αφροδίτης, seem to refer to what motivated Protesilaus' desire to return from the Underworld and the persistence of Laodamia's passionate love after her husband's death rather than to the cause of his death at Troy.

NOTES

¹ E.g., two recent books on Tibullus take the idea of *persona* for granted: D. F. Bright, *Haec Mihi Fingebam: Tibullus in his World* (Leiden 1978) 1, n. 1: "Any appreciation of Roman elegy rests on the distinction between recitation of experience, and the creation of an artistic world which purports to recite such experience"; and F. Cairns, *Tibullus: A Hellenistic Poet at Rome* (Cambridge 1979) speaks of *persona* throughout.

² A. S. F. Gow, *Theocritus* Vol. 2 (Cambridge 1952) 33, observes these features of the poem, concluding, "These points are touched in very lightly, but T. has made it plain that the liaison was likely to mean much more to the one than to the other."

³ For general examinations of the influence of Hellenistic poetry on Latin love elegy, see: H. E. Butler and E. A. Barber, *The Elegies of Propertius* (Oxford 1933) xxxv-lxvi; A. A. Day, *The Origins of Latin Love-Elegy* (Oxford 1938) 14-26; G. Luck, *The Latin Love Elegy²* (London 1969) 25-46.

⁴ Although I consider 68 to be one poem, for convenience I will refer to lines 1-40 as 68a, lines 41-148 as 68b and lines 149-60 as 68c.

⁵ Generally it is assumed that Lesbia is being compared to Laodamia here. For a fuller discussion, see below pp. 30-31.

⁶ S. Baker, "Lesbia's Foot," *CPh* 55 (1960) 172; G. Lieberg, *Puella Divina* (Amsterdam 1962) 249; Quinn, 392. See above p. 17.

⁷ There have been several attempts to emend or otherwise explain away *verecundae*. See above, pp. 31-32 and n. 88.

⁸ This question has not been satisfactorily answered. E.g., F. Solmsen, "Catullus' Artistry in C. 68: a pre-Augustan subjective Love-Elegy," in *Monumentum Chiloniense* (Amsterdam 1975) 269: "These somber notes are a testimony to his personal honesty rather than to an incomplete control of the artistic and emotional material," or P. Levine, "Catullus c. 68: A New Perspective," *CSCA* 9 (1976) 73: "extramarital relationships arising from unrestrained passions entail frustrations and hazards, and, where there is infidelity, the aggrieved partner must be prepared to adopt a realistic attitude of enlightened tolerance." The first statement ignores that a poet may choose whatever he wishes to discuss and emphasize and that, in poetry, honesty is not an excuse for incomplete control of material. The second attributes to Catullus an attitude apparent nowhere else in the Lesbia poems without explaining adequately the incongruity of the sentiment in the context in poem 68. Quinn, 392-93, is on the right track: "The switch from illusion to an attempt to face facts is very moving. The transition seems abrupt, however, unless it somehow corresponds to the associational structure of 101-60, which follow the sequence, in reverse order, of 1-88."

⁹ The standard chronology was set by L. Schwabe, *Quaestionum Catullianarum* (Gissae 1862) 357-61. This places both the affair with Lesbia and the death of the brother before Catullus' journey to Bithynia on Memmius' staff in 57 B.C. The affair must have begun before the death of Metellus Celer in 59, and poem 68 represents a time between these two points, probably closer to 57. The identification of the woman in poem 68 as Lesbia has been challenged from time to time: E.g., M. Rothstein, "Catull und Lesbia," *Philologus* 78 (1922) 8-12; I. K. Horvath, "Chronologica Catulliana," *AAntHung* 8 (1960) 335-47; R. Heine, "Zu Catull c. 68," *Latomus* 34 (1975) 166-86.

¹⁰ For a survey of scholarship before 1900 see A. Kalb, *de duodeseptuagesimo carmine Catulli* (Ansbach 1900); more recent is W. Hering, "Beobachtungen zu Catull c. 68, 41-160," *ACD* 8 (1972) 31-61, who reviews scholarship from 1959-72. V. Cremona, "Il carme 68 di Catullo 'Carmen Dupliciter Duplex,'" *Aevum* 41 (1967) 246-79; and Levine, "A New Perspective," 61-88, provide numerous citations in their notes and therefore serve as excellent starting points for the bibliography on poem 68.

¹¹ Among the interpretative studies I have found most interesting and helpful are: G. Pennisi, "Il carme 68 di Catullo," *Emerita* 27 (1959) 89-109 and 213-38; C. Witke, *Enar-*

ratio Catulliana (Leiden 1968); D. Bright, "*Confectum Carmine Munus*: Catullus 68," *ICS* 1 (1976) 86-112; Levine, "A New Perspective"; and G. Williams, *Figures of Thought in Roman Poetry* (New Haven 1980) 50-61.

¹² I have not included a discussion of the structure of the poem since my interpretation does not depend on structural analysis. For a review of the various structural schemata that have been proposed see R. McClure, "The Structure of Catullus 68," *CSCA* 7 (1974) 215-29.

¹³ The problem of the addressee's name is a troublesome one. In 68a at lines 11 and 30 the MSS read *mali*, which could perhaps be a corruption of *Malli* or *Manli*. In 68b, however, at lines 41, 50 and 150 it appears more likely that the name is Allius. At line 66 *O* gives *allius* (with *manllius* in the margin) and *G* and *R* give *manlius*. (For lists of the manuscript readings see H. W. Prescott, "The Unity of Catullus LXVIII," *TAPhA* 71 [1940] 494; or T. P. Wiseman, *Cinna the Poet* [Leicester 1974] 88.) Separatists, of course, may simply take the path of least resistance and read forms of Mallius or Manlius in 68a and of Allius in 68b. I have followed, in part, F. Schoell, "Zu Catullus," *NJbb* 121 (1880) 472-73, who suggested *id mi, Alli*, at line 30 (*mi* being dative, not vocative). At line 11 Schoell suggested that an original *amice* had been replaced by *mi Alli*, probably through a marginal gloss, and subsequently corrupted to *mali*. I have retained *mi Alli* at line 11 and *mi, Alli*, at line 30. I recognize that it would be easier to read *Malli* or *Manli* at lines 11 and 30 and that the elision in *mi Alli* is harsh and awkward. Nevertheless I am not proposing to use the addressee's name as proof of unity, but rather my interpretation of the poem insists on unity and therefore one addressee. Among supporters of this modification of Schoell's conjecture are: G. Perrotta, "L'elegia di Catullo ad Allio," *A&R* ser. 2, 8 (1927) 135-37; Prescott, "Unity," 493-97; Fordyce, 342; Lieberg, *Puella Divina* 153-54; Bright, "*Confectum Carmine Munus*," 88-90. Lachmann in his edition (Berlin 1829) used forms of *Manius* and *Allius*. The use of both *praenomen* and *nomen gentile* interchangeably is unusual, and nowhere else in the Catullan corpus is the *praenomen* used alone. Adherents of Lachmann's theory include: H. Magnus, "Die Einheit von Catulls Gedicht 68," *NJbb* 111 (1875) 850; A. Kiessling, *Analecta Catulliana* (Greifswald 1877) 15; J. Vahlen, "Ueber Catull's Elegie an M' Allius," *Sitz. der K. Preus. Akademie d. Wissenschaften zu Berlin* 44 (1902) 1024-25; L. Jus, "*de duodeseptuagesimo carmine Catulli*," *Eos* 30 (1927) 79-84; Witke, *Enarratio* 33, n. 1; B. Coppel, *Das Alliusgedicht* (Heidelberg 1973) 133-35; Mynors, in his OCT edition. Ellis, 401-402, suggested a double *nomen* or a *nomen gentile* used as a *praenomen*, i.e., Mallius Allius, but this solution seems contrived and the use of both *nomina* in one poem is no more likely than the use of *praenomen* and *nomen* would be. Pennisi, "Il carme 68," 228-35, emends to appropriate forms of Manlius at lines 11, 30, 41 and 66 and to forms of *ille* in lines 50 and 150. Thus line 50 reads *in deserto illi nomine opus faciat*, and line 150 *pro multis illis redditur officiis*. The dissonance of this line mars what otherwise seems to be an ingenious conjecture. Levine, "A New Perspective," 71-72, considers 68 a unified composition, whether one poem or two, and suggests that Allius of 68b is different from Mallius of 68a. 68b, he says, "is not about Mallius but for Mallius." The interpretation of the poem offered here reaches conclusions which differ greatly from Levine's and make his solution, for me, unacceptable. For the most recent and detailed critical text see D. F. S. Thomson, *Catullus. A Critical Edition* (Chapel Hill 1978).

¹⁴ These observations argue against any theory that Allius' misfortune is not love related: e.g., serious illness (Schoell, "zu Catullus," 472) or publical scandal (O. Harnecker, *Das 68. Gedicht des Catull* [Friedeberg 1881] 3-8). Coppel, *Das Aliusgedicht* 30-33, suggests that the real core of Allius' complaint is Catullus' absence from Rome and that lack of romantic attachment is only incidental to the main problem.

¹⁵ This is essentially the interpretation of Kalb, *de duodeseptuagesimo carmine* 34. Few regard the phrase *munera et Musarum et Veneris* as indicating a request for only one thing, a poem with erotic content: E.g., Baehrens, 493-95 and 501-503, who does not consider 68b to be the requested elegy since this would involve a contradiction on Catullus' part; and, Lieberg, *Puella Divina* 154-77, who suggests an epyllion, for which 68b is a substitute. It is unlikely that one would request anything as elaborate as an epyllion, which would require a long period of time to compose. *munera Musarum* must refer to poetry of some kind, but

munera Veneris is more difficult. One suggestion is that learned poetry is being distinguished from erotic: E.g., Magnus, "Einheit," 850-51; Kiessling, *Analecta* 14-15; Schoell, "Zu Catullus," 471; G. Jachmann, rev. of Kroll's edition, *Gnomon* 1 (1925) 211; Perrotta, "L'elegia," 138; E. Fraenkel, rev. of Fordyce's commentary, *Gnomon* 34 (1962) 262. This distinction seems artificial since all poetry should be subsumed under the rubric *munera Musarum*. There have been more corporeal interpretations of *munera Veneris*. F. Skutsch, "Zum 68. Gedicht Catulls," in *Kleine Schriften* (Leipzig 1914) 53-54; and K. Barwick, "Catulls c. 68 und eine Kompositionsform der roemischen Elegie," *WJA* 2 (1947) 2, see the phrase as a request that Catullus procure a woman for his friend, either through a letter of recommendation or direct intervention. Vahlen, "Catull's Elegie," 1025-29, explains that Allius, ignorant of Catullus' reasons for lingering in Verona and thinking he had abandoned Lesbia, was seeking permission to initiate an affair with her. Horvath, "Chronologica," 340-47, argues that Catullus and Allius had been sharing a Veronese girl and that in Catullus' absence Allius had been unable to keep her affection and so wanted Catullus to return to set things straight. Wiseman, *Cinna* 93-96, thinks that Catullus is being asked to share his mistress, a practice Wiseman asserts was commonplace at the time. T. E. Kinsey, "Some Problems in Catullus 68," *Latomus* 26 (1967) 38-42, suggests that Allius was interested in a homosexual affair with Catullus! None of these interpretations of *munera Veneris* can be gotten out of the text and the more general, if less sensational, interpretation I have cited above seems preferable. The poet's vagueness on these matters may well be intentional. Since what is of importance in the poem is Catullus' mental state, not Allius', he may wish not to detract from the main focus by providing too much detail about Allius.

¹⁶ H. A. J. Munro, *Criticisms and Elucidations of Catullus* (Cambridge 1878) 170; A. Palmer, "Ellis's Catullus," *Hermathena* 6 (1879) 346-47; Ellis, 401; F. Guglielmino, "Sulla composizione del carme LXVIII di Catullo," *Athenaeum* 3 (1915) 428; Perrotta, "L'elegia," 137; F. della Corte, *Due Studi Catulliani* (Genoa 1951) 131-42. The word *caelibe* in line 6 need not mean anything more than "alone": Kroll, 220-21; Pennisi, "Il carme 68," 100-103; *ThLL* II 65-66.

¹⁷ Coppel, *Das Alliusgedicht* 15-33, esp. 31-33, reads these lines as conscious exaggeration. He compares the tone of the opening of 68 with that of poem 50, addressed to Licinius Calvus. In that poem various symptoms of physical distress are piled one upon the other, yet the poem itself is ultimately light-hearted.

¹⁸ *vita* has been accepted almost universally as the correct reading here, and taken as a reference to Allius' beloved. So far as I know, Palmer, "Ellis's Catullus," 349, is alone in arguing that *tua vita* is not a reference to a woman but simply means "your life" literally. Perrotta, "L'elegia," 149-50, emends to *mea vita* and understands a reference to Lesbia.

¹⁹ Levine, "A New Perspective," 67, makes this point: "The conspicuous lack of sympathy in Catullus' response makes it most improbable that his friend lost a wife or girl friend through death."

²⁰ Examples of the former usage occur in Catull., 17.17; 61.204; 68.156. For examples from other authors see Kroll, 121. For the latter usage, Catull., 50.2. See also, H. Wagenvoort, *Studies in Roman Literature, Culture and Religion* (Leiden 1956) 30-42.

²¹ Observed by Lenchantin, 211.

²² Coppel, *Das Alliusgedicht* 51-52.

²³ Observed by M. Skinner, "The Unity of Catullus 68: The Structure of 68a," *TAPhA* 103 (1972) 501-502.

²⁴ I follow Lenchantin, 212-13 and Cremona, "Il carme 68," 248-49, in retaining the vocative *Catulle* and emending to *tepefecit*. (I differ from them, however, in reading *mi, Alli* at line 30.) Everything from *Veronae* to *cubili* then is direct discourse. Although the passage has been much discussed, the actual number of interpretations is limited. Baehrens, 497-99; and Kroll, 223, taking the passage as indirect statement and emending *Catulle* to *Catullo*, explain that it constitutes a reproach to Catullus for lingering in Verona (*hic*) where suitable romantic adventures could not be undertaken and one could merely try to warm cold limbs in an empty bed. Wiseman, *Cinna* 96-100, concurs with this interpretation but suggests that *Veronae turpe Catulle esse* is direct quotation, while the rest of lines 28

and 29 are paraphrase. Munro, *Criticisms* 172-74; Ellis, 406-407; Vahlen, "Catull's Elegie," 1027, and others view the passage as a description of Lesbia's conduct in Catullus' absence, i.e., it is disgraceful for Catullus to be in Verona when Lesbia is entertaining all the men of quality in Rome of Baiae (*hic*) in the bed that Catullus has abandoned. T. Birt, *de Catulli ad Mallium epistola commentariolum* (Marburg 1890) 11-12, thought that at issue was the condition of the addressee and other young men of Verona since Catullus had ceased to procure women from Rome for them! In this interpretation both *Veronae* and *hic* designate the addressee's location. Birt's theory has been modified by others, e.g., Horvath, "Chronologica," 345-47, who argues that Allius is speaking of his own condition since Catullus has left and he has lost the affection of the Veronese girl whose favors the friends were sharing. A. von Mess, "Dass 68. Gedicht Catulls und seine Stellung in der Geschichte der Elegie," *RhM* 63 (1908) 492, took the lines to be an exaggerated generalization: Catullus, the poet of love, is not in Rome to be heard and enjoyed by all, and those who miss him are languishing. Recently Coppel, *Das Allius-gedicht* 26-33, also argued that the lines characterize the condition of the young men of Catullus' circle in Rome, who are lost without their spiritual leader. Coppel makes the observation that *deserto* in line 29 should be taken in conjunction with *desertum* in line 6 and therefore considered a reference to Allius' condition.

[25] Some commentators see poem 38 as being completely serious, e.g., Ellis, 137, who suggests that Catullus was suffering from bodily as well as mental depression. F. Copley, "Catullus c. 38," *TAPhA* 87 (1956) 125-29, thinks Catullus is in mourning. Fordyce, 182, merely speaks of some kind of unspecified mental distress. The repetitions and exclamations, in particular line 2, *malest, me hercule, et laboriose*, should encourage the reader to consider the likelihood of a humorous exaggeration of Catullus' affliction and of Cornificius' dereliction. S. Baker, "Catullus 38," *CPh* 55 (1960) 37-38, observes the humor of line 2 but still insists on the overall seriousness of the poem. The final request for something sadder than Simonidean tears (7-8):

> *paulum quid lubet allocutionis*
> *maestius lacrimis Simonideis.*

seems so overstated as to assure us that the intent of the poem is light-hearted. Quinn, 206, warns against "supposing him on his deathbed or even prostrate with overwhelming grief."

[26] Baehrens, 499-500; Prescott, "Unity," 485-86; and Fordyce, 348, believe that the *copia scriptorum* contained works to which Catullus would need to refer in order to produce the learned poem Allius had requested. It seems unlikely, however, that one in grief, actual or imagined, would request a poem of such complexity.

[27] The interpretation of the poem offered here demands that 68 be a unity and therefore precludes the possibility that 68b was one of the poems in the *capsula* and subsequently accompanied 68a to Allius. Thus della Corte, *Due Studi* 137-38; F. Copley, "The Unity of Catullus 68: A Further View," *CPh* 52 (1957) 29-32.

[28] Observed by Levine, "A New Perspective," 70.

[29] Some take *non utriusque* as an indication that Catullus is fulfilling one of the two requests: e.g., W. Hoerschelmann, *de Catulli carmine duodeseptuagesimo* (Dorpat 1889) 15-16; and Skutsch, "Zum 68. Gedicht," 52-54. Others take the position I take here that Catullus says he can fulfill no part of the request: e.g., Birt, *commentariolum* 14; and Coppel, *Das Alliusgedicht*, 96. The Latin is ambiguous and admits of either interpretation, as is noted by Baehrens, 500-501; Lenchantin, 214; and Kroll, 225.

[30] Perrotta, "L'elegia," 138; R. Godel, "Catulle, Poème 68," *MH* 22 (1965) 53.

[31] Fordyce, 348-49, observes that although the usual convention is that the Muses speak to the poet, who then speaks to others, it is not unprecedented for the poet to ask the Muses to speak to others. He cites Callim., *Dian.* 3.186 and Theoc. *Id.* 22.116 as examples.

[32] Kinsey, "Some Problems," 46, n. 3, sees *carta anus* as an ironic allusion to the *multiloqua anus* of Roman comedy. I do not see the point of such irony here. Cf. *Ciris* 41: *nostra tuum senibus loqueretur pagina saeclis* (cited by Kroll, 226).

[33] A. G. Robson, "Catullus 68.53: The Coherence and Force of Tradition," *TAPhA* 103 (1972) 433-39, argues cogently for emending to *Trachinia rupes* in line 53. My observation about the tone of the passage would be unaffected by adoption of his suggestion.

[34] *Il.* 2.484-86. But Kroll, 226: "Die Musen kennen C.'s Leiden, da er sie ihnen durch seine Lieder anvertraut hat."

[35] I accept the reading of the MSS *corruerit* as do Ellis, 414, and Kroll, 226, rather than the usual emendation *torruerit. arderem* alone is sufficient to justify the heat images of lines 53-54, and *corruerit* provides a link between Catullus and Laodamia, who is cast down from a pinnacle of love (107-108).

[36] So F. Klingner in *L'Influence grecque sur la poésie latine de Catulle à Ovide* (Geneva 1953) 52. The question of whether the simile modifies Catullus' tears or Allius' *auxilium* has been much discussed. H. Offermann, "Der Flussvergleich bei Catull C. 68, 57ff.," *Philologus* 119 (1975) 57-69, argues for taking the simile with what follows for a number of reasons: 1) similar river similes in Theoc., *Id.* 1.7ff. and Verg., *Ecl.* 5.81ff. describe essentially pleasant things and so we should expect the simile here to refer to something pleasant, i.e., Allius' *auxilium* rather than Catullus' tears. The validity of this approach is questionable; 2) correspondences between the description of Catullus' condition in 51-56 and that of the river in 57-62 are not sufficient to warrant taking the simile with what precedes it. Offermann does not, however, demonstrate that there are more telling correspondences with the description of Allius' assistance that follows. Furthermore, Ellis, 412, and recently in much greater detail, J. Phillips, "The Pattern of Images in Catullus 68.51-62," *AJPh* 97 (1976) 340-43, show that the river simile does in fact bear a close relationship to the six lines that precede it; 3) the two similes, 57-62 and 63-65, correspond to two different aspects of Catullus' condition as described in lines 51-56. The *levamen* of the stream in the first simile relieves his *ardor* (*arderem*, 53) and the *aura secunda* of the second rescues him from the *imber* (56). F. Skutsch, "Zum 68. Gedicht," 49-50, whom Offermann cites, used this third observation to support his argument based on structure (pp. 46-49), but one could accept his structural analysis and the efficacy of this observation without insisting that the simile describe only Allius' *auxilium*. Another argument for taking the simile with what follows it is that thus *tale* of line 66 complements *qualis* of line 57 (Ellis, 412, *et al.*). The strongest argument for taking the simile with Catullus' tears is simply the sequence of ideas as they occur in the poem. It is perfectly natural to assume that the stream following immediately upon the tears should modify the tears. The simile may have been influenced by Hom. *Id.* 9.14-15, where Agamemnon's tears are described in an extended river simile. Fordyce, 350, further observes that the three other similes in Catullus which begin with *qualis* describe what precedes them (64.89; 65.13 and 68.109, although this last also modifies two different things). None of the arguments advanced on either side of the question prevent our understanding the simile to modify both the tears and the *auxilium*.

[37] E.g., Hom. *Il.* 13.487-95 and 17.722-34; Ap. Rh. *Argon.* 2.70-78 and 3.967-72.

[38] C. W. Macleod, "A Use of Myth in Ancient Poetry," *CQ* 24 (1974) 83, observes that there is a relationship between the two similes. This correspondence together with the mention of Troy serves to link Catullus with Laodamia; in fact, after the second lament for the dead brother, it is Catullus, not Lesbia, who is to be compared with Laodamia. See above, pp. 26-30.

[39] I read with Skutsch, "Zum 68. Gedicht," 50, and Mynors in his Oxford edition, *ac* for the *hec* of *O* (*R* and *G* have *hic*), not merely to allow the river simile to be taken with Allius' *auxilium* but to allow it to describe Catullus' tears as well.

[40] As far as I know, S. Johnson, "A Fresh Solution of a Famous Crux in Catullus," *CJ* (1944-45) 15-18, is alone in taking line 67 literally as a "field enclosed with a wide boundary wall, i.e., a suburban estate walled in, on which the villa of the rendezvous was situated." It is not clear that *domus* is appropriate for identifying a *villa suburbana*.

[41] I retain the reading of the MSS *dominam* but reject the idea that it refers to Lesbia, as Friedrich, 460; and Lieberg, *Puella Divina* 178-79, argue. Most who take the word to refer to Catullus' mistress emend to the dative *dominae* (e.g., Baehrens, 510; Kroll, 228; Lenchantin, 217; P. E. Streuli, *Die Lesbia-Partien in Catulls Allius-Elegie* [Urnaesch 1969] 1-4;

Quinn, 384; R. J. Baker, *"Domina* at Catullus 68, 68: Mistress or Chatelaine?" *RhM* 118 [1975] 124-29). The arguments against this interpretation are as follows: 1) it is not clear that *domina* was used of one's mistress this early (Lucil., fr. 708 [Krenkel], *cum mei adeunt servuli non dominam ego appellem meam*, is hard to interpret without a context.). Catullus uses it nowhere else. Unless *domina* for one's mistress were common, the reader would surely understand it to mean the mistress of the house. 2) the balance of the line is thrown off by having a dative here (J. P. Postgate, "Catulliana," *JPh* 17 [1889] 252; Prescott, "Unity," 489), and *nobis* would already include the person indicated by *dominae*. 3) if *dominae* (or *dominam*) refers to Catullus' mistress, *quam* of line 69 must have *domum* as its antecedent. Ellis, 415, notes that it is not unprecedented for the more distant possibility to be the antecedent. Fordyce, 351, observes that "The Latin for 'the house in which' is not *domus ad quam* but *domus in qua*." If *dominam* is mistress of the house, *ad quam* is easily explained as equivalent to *apud quam* (for examples see Ellis, 415). E. Baehrens, "Vier Verbesserungen zu Catullus," *NJbb* 117 (1878) 770, and Friedrich, 460, emend to *ad quem*, the *quem* having as its antecedent *is*. There is nothing to indicate, however, that the house is Allius'. Horvath, "Chronologica," 343-44, and Kinsey, "Some Problems," 43-44, take *dominam* as referring to a woman (not Lesbia) whom Catullus and Allius were sharing and explain *ad quam* in conjunction with *exerceremus communes amores*; Allius and Catullus, they say, exercised the love they had in common for this woman. 4) the mention of Lesbia here serves no particular function and would only detract from her appearance in line 70 as *candida diva* (so Postgate, "Catulliana," 252, and Ellis, 414-15). To be sure, Lesbia must be included in *exerceremus* (69), but she is not brought forth vividly and in person there. 5) as L. P. Wilkinson, *"Domina* in Catullus 68," *CR* n.s. 20 (1970) 290, argues, in line 156 *domus* and *domina* again appear together, and since Lesbia must be the *lux mea* of line 160, she cannot be the *domina* of line 156. It follows then that she cannot be the *dominam* of line 68 either. This argument depends, however, on how one completes and interprets line 156 (see above, p. 37).

⁴² Kroll, 229; Prescott, "Unity," 491; Lenchantin, 217; Fordyce, 352. *communes* would thus have the force of *mutuos* as in Lucr. 4.1195-96 and 1207. Horvath, "Chronologica," 341-44; Kinsey, "Some Problems," 43-44; and Heine, "Zu Catull c. 68," 169, offer variations on the idea that the phrase refers to the sharing of a mistress by Catullus and Allius. It is hard to see how such an arrangement would have relieved Catullus' distress as described in lines 51-56, and it seems highly likely that the woman in question is Lesbia (consider line 160, *lux mea qua viva vivere dulce mea est*). It is incredible to me that the poet would have labored over poem 68 as he must have to treat of a casual *ménage à trois*. Perhaps the explanation of Ellis, 415, that Allius and Catullus are the subjects of *exerceremus* and the *communes amores* are the love each had for his own mistress is more plausible, although Allius' love affair, prominent in 68a, has all but been forgotten by Catullus at this point in the poem.

⁴³ Observed by Levine, "A New Perspective," 72, but his interpretation that "the playfulness that Catullus displays...in his exaltation of an act of *hospitium* that, if taken seriously, should serve rather to stigmatize than to immortalize the memory of the benefactor subtly reveals a brightening of mood..." is not at all in accord with mine.

⁴⁴ Lieberg, *Puella Divina* 191-94, sees a difference in meaning between *diva* and *dea*, but Kroll, 229, feels that the meter is the only determining factor.

⁴⁵ Streuli, *Lesbia-Partien* 25-26.

⁴⁶ Streuli, *Lesbia-Partien* 29-32.

⁴⁷ Ellis, 415.

⁴⁸ Apparently she is wearing a wooden-soled sandal (the kind described in Isid. *Orig.* 19.34.11), which would leave her foot exposed and the sole of which would make the sound indicated by *arguta*. Fordyce, 352, offers some possible meanings for *arguta*.

⁴⁹ Plaut. *Cas.* 815-16; Catull. 61.159-61; Plut. *Quaest. Rom.* 29.

⁵⁰ I am essentially following S. Baker, "Lesbia's Foot," 171-73, on the idea that the stepping on the threshold was a sign of ill-omen. He seems to me, however, to go too far in suggesting (p. 172) that Lesbia's action "may be an impudent flouting of both marriage and divine Luck." There is no reason to believe that Catullus or Lesbia would have been

concerned with such a superstition at the time of their meeting. It is only in the context of the poem that the meeting takes on the symbolic force of a marriage and only there that the ill-omened act has significance. Lieberg, *Puella Divina* 207-209, suggests that the detail of Lesbia's stepping on the threshold may be intended to confirm what is later stated clearly (143-46), that Catullus' relationship with Lesbia is not a legitimate marriage. Streuli, *Lesbia-Partien* 36-37, opposes this idea but not very persuasively. My objection to Lieberg's suggestion is that avoidance of the threshold seems to have had nothing to do with legitimizing the marriage but with ensuring the prosperity of the union.

⁵¹ For discussions of the ancient accounts of the Laodamia myth, see: E. Baehrens, "Die Laodamiasage und Catulls 68s Gedicht," *NJbb* 115 (1877) 409-15; Roscher, *Lex.* ii. 1827-28; Lieberg, *Puella Divina* 209-18; and H. Jacobson, *Ovid's Heroides* (Princeton 1974) 195ff. For a thoughtful discussion of the function of the myth in poem 68, see Macleod, "A Use of Myth," 82-88. For an assessment of the variations readers of poem 68 would have been expected to know, see the Appendix.

⁵² Hom. *Il.* 2.698-702; Apollod. *Epit.*, 3.30; Hyg. *Fab.* 103; Lucian *Dial. Mort.* 23; Servius *ad Aen.* 6, 447; Tzetz. *Antehomerica* 246-49; *Schol. Aristid.* (Dindorf, Vol. 3) p. 671.

⁵³ Tzetz. *Chil.* 2.777-80; perhaps also Paus. 4.2.7, where the account given in the *Cypria* is cited.

⁵⁴ There is disagreement as to who initiates the request for Protesilaus' return. Hyg., *Fab.* 103; and Servius, *ad Aen.* 6.447, say that Laodamia made the request. Lucian, *Dial. Mort.* 23; *Schol. Aristid.* p. 671; and Eust. *Il.* 325, say that Protesilaus did. Tzetz. *Chil.* 2. 762-67, says that Persephone herself, unprompted by either, made the suggestion.

⁵⁵ Apollod. *Epit.* 3.30; Hyg. *Fab.* 103; Eust. *Il.* 325; Tzetz. *Chil.* 2.770-76.

⁵⁶ Apollod. *Epit.* 3.30; Eust. *Il.* 325.

⁵⁷ Macleod, "A Use of Myth," 85-86, observes this emphasis.

⁵⁸ R. F. Thomas, "An Alternative to Ceremonial Negligence (Catullus 68. 73-78)," *HSPh* 82 (1978) 175-78, suggests that lines 75-76, *nondum cum sanguine sacro / hostia caelestis pacificasset eros*, refers not to neglect by Laodamia or Protesilaus but to the sacrifice of Iphigenia. He does not mention lines 79-80, which seem to make it clear that Laodamia is being punished because the altars have been slighted.

⁵⁹ Williams, *Figures* 51, sees here what he calls "arbitrary assertion of similarity," requiring the reader to wait until more information is available before determining the significance of the simile.

⁶⁰ The commentators do not indicate that they consider the apostrophe at all extraordinary. E.g., Quinn, 386: "Translated into non-heroic terms, this means that C. prays that he will never, to gain gratification of desire, embark precipately upon a course of action which is doomed to disaster." L. Pepe, "Il mito di Laodamia nel carme 68 di Catullo," *GIF* 6 (1953) 112, not only takes the lines as a serious statement but seems to believe that Catullus was actually afraid of the goddess Nemesis. Kinsey, "Some Problems," 51, n. 2, is puzzled by the lines and asks if they might constitute Catullus' assertion that he will not act contrary to Lesbia's wishes. He observes that Lesbia is called *diva* a few lines earlier and *era* later in the poem. In this case the apostrophe may have a bearing on Catullus' resolution that he will tolerate Lesbia's infidelity (135-37).

⁶¹ Lenchantin, 138, says of 63.91-93 to which he refers in his discussion of this passage (p. 218): "Il voto corrisponde allo stile della poesia ellenistica." Fordyce, 353, also compares the two passages. He calls 63.91-93 a personal prayer (p. 271), citing Callim. *Cer.* 136f. and *Dem.* 116f.

⁶² I do not agree with Kinsey, "Some Problems," 50, n. 4, that "the sin is attributed to Laudamia in order to enable Catullus to indulge in sarcasm at the gods' expense." The "prosaic" *ieiuna* does not seem to me contemptuous as it does to Kinsey.

⁶³ Pepe, "Il mito," 110-13, sees in Laodamia's neglect of the gods an acknowledgment on Catullus' part of the illicit nature of his own affair with Lesbia. Pennisi, "Il carme 68," 217, argues against this idea. If the distinction between poet and Catullus is maintained, Pepe's view is not inconsistent with my observations that throughout the poem the poet undercuts Catullus' lofty assertions and rationalizations concerning his love affair with hints about the actual and less than ideal situation.

⁶⁴ Kinsey, "Some Problems," 50.

⁶⁵ The emendation of Heinsius for *que vetet id* of the MSS is generally accepted. There are many examples of *-ne* added to the relative pronoun (e.g., Catull. 64.180, *quemne ipsa reliqui*; Hor. *Sat.* 1.10.21). This practice is especially common in Plautus (e.g., *Mil.* 13 and 614 and *Merc.* 573). Ellis, 419, feeling that *quaene* is too colloquial, proposes *qualiter*. But if the lament is supposed to be a sudden eruption of spontaneous emotion by Catullus, a colloquialism would not be inconsistent.

⁶⁶ But Prescott, "Unity," 475, n. 4, sees in the repetition "evidence of the depth and sincerity of Catullus' grief." Most disagree with Prescott and hence the attempts to explain away the second lament.

⁶⁷ I reject all theories that make these lines an addition to an already completed poem. J. Wohlberg, "The Structure of the Laodamia Simile in Catullus 68b," *CPh* 50 (1955) 42-46; K. Vretska, "Das Problem der Einheit von Catull c. 68," *WS* 79 (1966) 323-28; and Wiseman, *Cinna* 70-76, present structural schemes for the Laodamia passage that work only if lines 91-100 are omitted. They then argue that this passage, which disrupts their patterns, must have been added after the poem had been completed. Copley, "Unity," 29-32, reaches the same conclusion based on content rather than on structure, and Godel, "Poème 68," 63, makes similar observations. Guglielmino, "composizione," 440-42, suggests that most of 68b was written first, and that after composing 68a (for a different addressee) the poet added some passages, including the repeated lines, to 68b. della Corte, *Due Studi* 134-42, modifies this view. He believes that 68b was sent to the addressee of 68a and suggests that the echoes and repetitions were placed in 68a from 68b to give the verse epistle a more lively and cordial tone. I cannot accept that in a poem as complex and elaborate as 68 (or even just 68b) the poet would destroy whatever he was attempting to convey by inserting lines into a finished poem. It is one thing to make a critical judgment that the poem reads better with or without certain lines and quite another to deny the poet the awareness to realize what he is trying to say and the control over his material to say it. T. Frank, "A Rejected Poem and a Substitute: Catullus LXVIII A and B," *AJPh* 35 (1914) 67-73, suggests that 68a was never intended for publication and that therefore the problem of the repetition arose only because 68a was published by an editor after Catullus' death.

⁶⁸ Luck, *Love Elegy* 62, by his translation, "cherished apple of my eye," indicates that he understands *lumen* in this way. *lumen* as light of life, however, is so widely accepted that most discussions of this section of the poem do not even contain comment on the word.

⁶⁹ Williams, *Figures* 55; also, C. J. Tuplin, "Catullus 68," *CQ* 31 (1981) 118.

⁷⁰ On my emendation *tandem* here, see above p. 28 and n. 77 below.

⁷¹ Commentators invariably interpret the word to mean "whirlpool." E.g., Ellis, 420-21; Kroll, 233; Fordyce, 355. The only virtue of this interpretation, it seems to me, is that *vertice* as "whirlpool" strengthens the force of *absorbens*.

⁷² See Tuplin, "Catullus 68," 119-31, for a detailed examination of possible sources for the treatment of the *barathrum* here. He concludes that the poet was influenced by a passage from Euphorion's *Chiliades*.

⁷³ Lenchantin, 221.

⁷⁴ Ellis, 285.

⁷⁵ Tuplin, "Catullus 68," 120.

⁷⁶ See *ThLL* II 1723-24. Plaut. *Bacch.* 149-51:

> *o barathrum, ubi nunc es? ut ego te usurpem libens!*
> *video nimio iam multo plus quam volueram;*
> *vixisse nimio satiust iam quam vivere.*

Tuplin, "Catullus 68," 138-39, provides an appendix with a detailed list of metaphorical uses of the word.

⁷⁷ Kroll, 235, emends the unmetrical *tuum domitum* of the MSS to *tunc indomitam*. It seems clear that the object of *docuit* must be either Laodamia herself or Protesilaus. The latter possibility, however, is not particularly appropriate since throughout the passage it has been Laodamia's love and grief that have been emphasized. Thus any emendation

that retains *domitum* or substitutes another masculine form (as, e.g., do Baehrens, 523-25 and Ellis, 423) must be rejected. The emendation *tamen* (Heinsius) is supported by Munro, *Criticisms* 189-90; Mynors in his Oxford edition; and Fordyce, 356. Reading *tamen* or *tunc* instead of *tandem* does not affect my interpretation of the passage. Lenchantin, 222, offers: *qui tantum domitam ferre iugum docuit.*

[78] The clearest indication that the metaphor had become a common idiom comes from Plaut., *Curc.* 50-52:

> PA(linurus). *iamne ea fert iugum?*
> PH(aedromus). *tam a me pudica est quasi soror mea sit,*
> *nisi si est osculando quippiam inpudicior.*

Baehrens, 523-25, cites other examples.

[79] Kroll, 235, cites this word used twice by Homer, *Od.* 6.109 and 228. Also Fordyce, 356. Munro, *Criticisms* 189, is correct in insisting that Laodamia must be the one who bears the yoke but not in rendering *indomitam* as "indomitable."

[80] Observed by Lenchantin, 222. D. Braga, *Catullo e i Poeti Greci* (Messina 1950) cites only a few passages in his chapter on the relations of Catullus and Pindar but surprisingly does not mention this passage.

[81] On the dove's faithfulness to its mate, Prop. 2.15.27-28; Pliny, *HN* 10.104; Porphyr. *ad Hor. epod.* 16.32.

[82] Streuli, *Lesbia-Partien* 39-42, argues for the reading *paulum* here.

[83] E.g., Ellis, 426; Fordyce, 358; Williams, *Figures* 51, who notes "the qualification must be disturbing." All assume, of course, that the comparison is between Lesbia and Laodamia.

[84] Streuli, *Lesbia-Partien* 91-92.

[85] Kroll, 237; Lieberg, *Puella Divina* 246-48.

[86] Streuli, *Lesbia-Partien* 96-97, explains *furta* as referring to Lesbia's marriage and reflecting entirely Catullus' perspective, that his relationship with her is proper, her husband's illegitimate. Since Lesbia then acts out of obligation to her husband, she may still be called *verecunda.*

[87] See Fordyce, 358, on Catullus' references to himself by name.

[88] Ellis, 426; Kroll, 237; and Fordyce, 358, justify *verecundae* by the fact that the *furta* are *rara.* As soon as one *furtum* is admitted, however, the adjective becomes inappropriate. Lieberg, *Puella Divina* 257-59, understands *verecundae* in the sense of "deserving respect" rather than "modest," and H. Reynen, "*Rara verecundae furta feremus erae* (Cat. 68, 136)," *MH* 31 (1974) 150-54, suggests that *verecunda* may be equivalent to the Greek πότνια. In either case the word would still imply that the one so described is worthy of respect as a result of proper conduct, and the incongruity would remain. J. B. Bauer, "*Erae furta verecundae* (Catull 68, 136)," *WS* n.f. 9 (1975) 78-82, and A. W. J. Holleman, "Lesbia as a *verecunda era* (Cat., 68, 136)," *RBPh* 56 (1978) 38-40, suggest that *verecunda* here means "discreet." K. Buechner, "Catull 68, 136," *MH* 7 (1950) 14-18, recognizing the incongruity of *verecundae*, would emend to the adverb *verecunde*, modifying *feremus.* Quinn, 393, asks the right question: "Does *verecundae* express a hope for the future or betray self-deception about the present?" and Williams, *Figures* 58, calls *verecundae* "a surprising, even contradictory, and so, wishful, word to use."

[89] Streuli, *Lesbia-Partien* 102-103. The passage he cites from Ovid *Her.* 9.78 uses *era* of a slave-mistress relationship. *era* there refers not to Deianeira as Streuli says but is used by Deianeira of Omphale.

[90] The MSS have *flagrantem quotidiana.* Streuli, *Lesbia-Partien* 52-59, provides a detailed summary of the problem and himself supports the most popular emendation, *flagrantem concoquit iram.* Also accepting this reading are Kroll, 230; Lenchantin, 223; and Fordyce, 359. Ellis, 426, suggests *contudit iram.*

[91] Friedrich, 473; Lenchantin, 224; and Quinn, 393-94, argue against assumption of a lacuna. Ellis, 427; Kroll, 238; Fordyce, 359; and Streuli, *Lesbia-Partien* 68-74, argue for one.

⁹² Although *mira* has been challenged, it seems to me to make perfect sense here. For a discussion of *mira* and proposed emendations see Streuli, *Lesbia-Partien*, 80-85.

⁹³ On reading *diem* instead of *dies* see Fordyce, 360 and Streuli, *Lesbia-Partien* 87-89.

⁹⁴ Ellis, 428; Fordyce, 395.

⁹⁵ Fordyce, 360, and Ellis, 429, draw from Pind. *Isthm.* 8.40ff., where Themis bestows the γέρας θεόμορον (i.e., Thetis) on Peleus for being εὐσεβέστατος.

⁹⁶ A word has fallen out in line 156, and the *deteriores* have *domus ipsa in qua, domus in qua nos*, and *domus in qua olim*. My preference for the first of these is simply that it adds emphasis to the slightly unusual personification of the house.

⁹⁷ On *vita*, see above n. 18.

⁹⁸ Prescott, "Unity," 491-93, contends that the house is Allius' and the *domina* his wife. Line 156 then becomes a restatement of line 155, and each of the last three couplets refers to one person or set of persons. The interpretation of Allius' distress I have offered, of course, precludes this possibility.

⁹⁹ Kinsey, "Some Problems," 45, advances a sound and persuasive argument in favor of this view. All explanations of the passage that introduce a new person into the poem at this point must be rejected. For detailed surveys of these numerous and sometimes extravagant suggestions see Johnson, "A Fresh Solution," 10-13, and Cremona, "Il carme 68," 258-64. Lenchantin, 225-26, takes *terram* as symbolic for rescue and emends to *terram dat et aufert*, referring to some person unknown to us. T. P. Wiseman, "Catullus 68.157," *CR* n.s. 24 (1974) 6-7, emends to *vobis me tradidit* with *aufert* concealing the name of the person who introduced Catullus to Allius. Vahlen, "Catull's Elegie," 1043, simply emends the *et* of line 157 to *dum* and reads the line as a reference to Jupiter indicating time ("solange es euch vergoennt ist"). Pennisi, "Il carme 68," 225-27, also takes the lines as a reference to Jupiter but transposes them to immediately after line 154. Likewise Vretska, "Das Problem der Einheit," 322-23, who would move the couplet to after line 140 and change the *et* of line 157 to *en*. Perrotta, "L'elegia," 146-51, makes the couplet refer to Allius by emending to:

> *et qui principio nobis se et eram dedit a quo*
> *sunt primo nobis omnia nata bona.*

APPENDIX NOTES

¹ For the fragments see Morel, *FPL*. H. de la Ville de Mirmont, *Études sur l'Ancienne Poésie Latine* (Paris 1903) 279-90, offers some good suggestions for a reconstruction.

² Anaxandrides (4th c. B.C.) wrote a comedy *Protesilaus*, from the fragments of which little, if anything, can be determined (Edmonds, *Fragments of Attic Comedy* [Leiden 1959] Vol. 2, 63-69). According to Stephan of Byzantium, *Ethnice* (under *Phylace*), a Heliodorus, (perhaps the novelist, fl. ca. 220-50 of our era) wrote a *Protesilaus*.

³ Although Parthenius' dedication of this work to Gallus (b. 69 B.C.) makes its date post-Catullan, the authors cited in it are Hellenistic.

⁴ But see Jacobson, *Heroides* 211.

BIBLIOGRAPHY

TEXTS AND COMMENTARIES

Catullus, Gaius Valerius, *Catulli Veronensis Liber*, ed. Emil Baehrens, Leipzig, 1885-93, 2 v.
——, *Catulli Veronensis Liber*, ed. Robinson Ellis, 2nd ed., Oxford, 1878.
——, *Catullus. A Commentary*, ed. C. J. Fordyce, Oxford, 1961.
——, *Catulli Veronensis Liber*, ed. Gustav Friedrich, Leipzig, 1908.
——, *C. Valerius Catullus*, ed. Wilhelm Kroll, 5th ed., Stuttgart, 1968.
——, *Q. Valerii Catulli Veronensis Liber*, ed. Karl Lachmann, Berlin, 1829.
——, *Il Libro di Catullo*, ed. Massimo Lenchantin de Gubernatis, Torino, 1953.
——, *C. Valerii Catulli Carmina*, ed. R. A. B. Mynors, Oxford, 1958.
——, *Catullus: The Poems*, ed. Kenneth Quinn, New York, 1970.
——, *Catullus. A Critical Edition*, ed. D. F. S. Thomson, Chapel Hill, 1978.
Edmonds, John Maxwell, *The Fragments of Attic Comedy*, Leiden, 1957-61, 4 v.
Ellis, Robinson, *A Commentary on Catullus*, 2nd ed., Oxford, 1889.
Ovidius Naso, Publius, *Amores, Medicamina Faciei Femineae, Ars Amatoria, Remedia Amoris*, ed. E. J. Kenney, Oxford, 1961.
——, *Epistulae Heroidum*, ed. Henricus Doerrie, Berlin, 1971.
Propertius, Sextus Aurelius, *The Elegies of Propertius*, ed. H. E. Butler and E. A. Barber, Oxford, 1933.
Theocritus, *Theocritus*, ed. A. S. F. Gow, Cambridge, 1952, 2 v.

BOOKS AND ARTICLES

Baehrens, Emil, "Die Laodamiasage und Catulls 68. Gedicht," *NJbb* 115 (1887) 409-15.
——, "Vier Verbesserungen zu Catullus," *NJbb* 117 (1878) 769-70.
Baker, Robert J., "*Domina* at Catullus 68, 68: Mistress or Chatelaine?" *RhM* 118 (1975) 124-29.
Baker, Sheridan, "Catullus 38," *CPh* 55 (1960) 37-38.
——, "Lesbia's Foot," *CPh* 55 (1960) 171-73.
Barwick, Karl, "Catulls c. 68 und eine Kompositionsform der roemischen Elegie und Epigrammatik," *WJA* 2 (1947) 1-15.
Bauer, J. B., "*Erae furta verecundae* (Catull 68, 136)," *WS* n.f. 9 (1975) 78-82.
Birt, Theodor, *de Catulli ad Mallium epistola commentariolum*, Marburg, 1890.
Braga, Domenico, *Catullo e i Poeti Greci*, Messina, 1950.
Bright, David F., "*Confectum Carmine Munus*: Catullus 68," *ICS* 1 (1976) 86-112.
——, *Haec Mihi Fingebam: Tibullus in his World*, Leiden, 1978. (Cincinatti Classical Studies, 3)
Buechner, Karl, "Catull 68, 136," *MH* 7 (1950) 14-18.
Cairns, Francis, *Tibullus: A Hellenistic Poet at Rome*, Cambridge, 1979.
Copley, Frank O., "Catullus c. 38," *TAPhA* 87 (1956) 125-29.
——, "The Unity of Catullus 68: A Further View," *CPh* 52 (1957) 29-32.
Coppel, Bernhard, *Das Alliusgedicht*, Heidelberg, 1973.
Corte, Francesco della, *Due Studi Catulliani*, Genoa, 1951, 131-42.
Cremona, Virginio, "Il carme 68 di Catullo '*Carmen Dupliciter Duplex*,' " *Aevum* 41 (1967) 246-79.
Day, Archibald A., *The Origins of Latin Love-Elegy*, Oxford, 1938.
Fraenkel, Eduard, review of *Catullus. A Commentary*, by C. J. Fordyce, *Gnomon* 34 (1962) 253-63.
Frank, Tenney, "A Rejected Poem and a Substitute: Catullus LXVIII A and B," *AJPh* 35 (1914) 67-73.

Godel, Robert, "Catulle, Poème 68," *MH* 22 (1965) 53-65.

Guglielmino, Francesco, "Sulla composizione del carme LXVIII di Catullo," *Athenaeum* 3 (1915) 426-44.

Harnecker, Otto, *Das 68. Gedicht des Catull*, Friedeberg, 1881.

Heine, Rolf, "Zu Catull c. 68," *Latomus* 34 (1975) 166-86.

Hering, Wolfgang, "Beobachtungen zu Catull c. 68, 41-160," *ACD* 8 (1972) 31-61.

Hoerschelmann, W., *de Catulli carmine duodeseptuagesimo*, Dorpat, 1889.

Holleman, A. W. J., "Lesbia as a *verecunda era* (Cat., 68, 136)," *RBPh* 56 (1978) 38-40.

Horvath, I. K., "Chronologica Catulliana," *AAntHung* 8 (1960) 335-68.

L'Influence grecque sur la Poésie latine de Catulle à Ovide, ed. Jean Bayet, Geneva, 1953.
    (Fondation Hardt Entretiens sur l'antiquité classique, 2)

Jachmann, Guenther, review of *C. Valerius Catullus*, herausgegeben und erklaert von Wilhelm Kroll, *Gnomon* 1 (1925) 200-14.

Jacobson, Howard, *Ovid's Heroides*, Princeton, 1974.

Johnson, S., "A Fresh Solution of a Famous Crux in Catullus," *CJ* 40 (1944-45) 10-18.

Jus, Ludovicus, "*de duodeseptuagesimo carmine Catulli*," *Eos* 30 (1927) 77-92 and 31 (1928) 63-77.

Kalb, Alfons, *de duodeseptuagesimo carmine Catulli*, Ansbach, 1900.

Kiessling, Adolf Gottlieb, *Analecta Catulliana*, Greifswald, 1877, 13-20.

Kinsey, T. E., "Some Problems in Catullus 68," *Latomus* 26 (1967) 35-53.

La Ville de Mirmont, Henri de, *Études sur l'Ancienne Poésie Latine*, Paris, 1903.

Levine, Philip, "Catullus c. 68: A New Perspective," *CSCA* 9 (1976) 61-88.

Lieberg, Godo, *Puella Divina*, Amsterdam, 1962, 152-263.

Luck, Georg, *The Latin Love Elegy*, 2nd ed., London, 1969.

Macleod, C. W., "A Use of Myth in Ancient Poetry," *CQ* 24 (1974) 82-93.

Magnus, Hugo, "Die Einheit von Catulls Gedicht 68," *NJbb* 111 (1875) 849-54.

Mess, Adolph von, "Das 68. Gedicht Catulls und seine Stellung in der Geschichte der Elegie," *RhM* 63 (1908) 488-94.

McClure, Robert, "The Structure of Catullus 68," *CSCA* 7 (1974) 215-29.

Munro, Hugh A. J., *Criticisms and Elucidations of Catullus*, Cambridge, 1878, 166-94.

Offermann, Helmut, "Der Flussvergleich bei Catull C. 68, 57ff.," *Philologus* 119 (1975) 57-69.

Palmer, Arthur, "Ellis's Catullus," *Hermathena* 6 (1879) 293-363.

Pennisi, Giuseppe, "Il carme 68 di Catullo," *Emerita* 27 (1959) 89-109 and 213-38.

Pepe, Luigi, "Il mito di Laodamia nel carme 68 di Catullo," *GIF* 6 (1953) 107-13.

Perrotta, Gennaro, "L'elegia di Catullo ad Allio," *A&R* ser. 2, 8 (1927) 134-51.

Phillips, Jane E., "The Pattern of Images in Catullus 68.51-62," *AJPh* 97 (1976) 340-43.

Postgate, J. P., "Catulliana," *JPh* 17 (1889) 226-67.

Prescott, Henry W., "The Unity of Catullus LXVIII," *TAPhA* 71 (1940) 473-500.

Reynen, Hans, "*Rara verecundae furta feremus erae* (Cat. 68, 136)," *MH* 31 (1974) 150-54.

Robson, Arthur G., "Catullus 68. 53: The Coherence and Force of Tradition," *TAPhA* 103 (1972) 433-39.

Rothstein, M., "Catull und Lesbia," *Philologus* 78 (1922) 1-34.

Schoell, Fritz, "Zu Catullus," *NJbb* 121 (1880) 471-80.

Schwabe, Ludwig von, *Quaestionum Catullianarum*, Gissae, 1862.

Skinner, Marilyn B., "The Unity of Catullus 68: The Structure of 68a," *TAPhA* 103 (1972) 495-512.

Skutsch, Franz, "Zum 68. Gedicht Catulls," in *Kleine Schriften*, Leipzig, 1914, 46-58. (Reprinted from *RhM* 47 [1892] 138-51.)

Solmsen, Friedrich, "Catullus' Artistry in C. 68: A pre-Augustan subjective Love-Elegy," in *Monumentum Chiloniense*, ed. by Eckard Lefèvre, Amsterdam, 1975.

Streuli, Peter Ernst, *Die Lesbia-Partien in Catulls Allius-Elegie*, Urnaesch, 1969.

Thomas, Richard F., "An Alternative to Ceremonial Negligence (Catullus 68. 73-78)," *HSPh* 82 (1978) 175-78.

Tuplin, C. J., "Catullus 68," *CQ* 31 (1981) 113-39.

Vahlen, Johannes, "Ueber Catull's Elegie an M. Allius," *Sitz. der K. Preussischen Akad. der Wissenschaften zu Berlin* 44 (1902) 1024-1043.

Vretska, Karl, "Das Problem der Einheit von Catull c. 68," *WS* 79 (1966) 313-30.

Wagenvoort, Hendrik, "*Ludus Poeticus*" in *Studies in Roman Literature, Culture, and Religion*, Leiden, 1956, 30-42.

Wilkinson, L. P., "*Domina* in Catullus 68," *CR* n.s. 20 (1970) 290.

Williams, Gordon, *Figures of Thought in Roman Poetry*, New Haven, 1980.

Wiseman, Timothy P., "Catullus 68. 157," *CR* n.s. 24 (1974) 6-7.

——, *Cinna the Poet*, Leicester, 1974.

Witke, Charles, *Enarratio Catulliana*, Leiden, 1968. (Mnemosyne Supplement, 10)

Wohlberg, Joseph, "The Structure of the Laodamia Simile in Catullus 68b," *CPh* 50 (1955) 42-46.

Printed in the United States
By Bookmasters